ENDGAME

FIELD NOTES

SERIES EDITOR: Paul Mattick

A series of books providing in-depth analyses of today's global turmoil as it unfolds. Each book focuses on an important feature of our present-day economic, political and cultural condition, addressing local and international issues. Field Notes examines the many dimensions of today's social predicament and provides a radical, politically and critically engaged voice to global debates.

Published in association with the *Brooklyn Rail*

Titles in the series:

Endgame: Economic Nationalism and Global Decline
JAMIE MERCHANT

A Happy Future is a Thing of the Past: The Greek Crisis and Other Disasters
PAVLOS ROUFOS

Hinterland: America's New Landscape of Class and Conflict
PHIL A. NEEL

No Home for You Here: A Memoir of Class and Culture
ADAM THERON-LEE RENSCH

Smart Machines and Service Work: Automation in an Age of Stagnation
JASON E. SMITH

States of Incarceration: Rebellion, Reform, and America's Punishment System
JARROD SHANAHAN AND ZHANDARKA KURTI

ENDGAME

*Economic Nationalism
and Global Decline*

JAMIE MERCHANT

REAKTION BOOKS

For my mother

Published by Reaktion Books Ltd
Unit 32, Waterside
44–48 Wharf Road
London N1 7UX, UK
www.reaktionbooks.co.uk

First published 2024
Copyright © Jamie Merchant 2024

Printed and bound in Great Britain by TJ Books Ltd, Padstow, Cornwall

A catalogue record for this book is available from the British Library

ISBN 978 1 78914 914 2

Contents

Yesterday the prayer to the sunset
And the adoration of madmen. But to-day the struggle.
—W. H. AUDEN, "SPAIN" (1937)

Introduction

It was a cloudy but pleasant mid-spring afternoon when a heavily armed teenager pulled into the parking lot of Tops supermarket in Buffalo, New York. Having already scouted the area the day before, he knew exactly what to do and where to go. After making the four-hour drive from Conklin to Buffalo, his plan was to get a quick meal at a nearby McDonald's. Replenished, he would pull into a quiet side street to suit up in full body armor and tactical combat helmet, and to prep a Bushmaster xM-15 assault rifle modified to carry high-capacity magazines. He would then return to the store, making sure to arrive at the busiest time of day. After running training exercises at home, he had calculated that kicking open the door of the car and opening fire would take about two seconds.

In what he described as a "partisan action against an occupying force," Payton Gendron murdered ten people, all of whom were Black, on May 14, 2022. According to the account of his actions published online shortly before the attack, as he browsed 4chan forums in mind-numbing boredom during the early months of the covID-19 pandemic, he had discovered an intricate conspiracy, perpetrated by a shadowy Jewish elite, to wipe out the "white race." A cascade of infographics and memes claimed to show how these elites were supposedly replacing lighter-skinned people of European descent, like him, with immigrants and Black people by pushing liberal immigration laws and lowering white birth rates. The more he read about it, the more despondent he felt. Who could hope to stand up to such a vast global conspiracy? Who could stop "race doom," as he referred to it? He eventually grew suicidal. Then he happened upon a video of Brenton Tarrant, the white supremacist shooter who killed 51 people, mostly Muslims, in Christchurch, New Zealand, in 2019. Shortly thereafter, he read about other such "fighters," like Anders Breivik, the Norwegian ultraright terrorist who murdered 77 people, including 69 young students, at a Workers' Youth League summer camp in 2011. Gendron had found his solution: instead of ending his own life, he too would become a fighter by targeting the "replacers" themselves. He too would "do something." Most importantly, he would make sure that his account on the live-streaming service Twitch broadcasted the live video feed from his helmet-mounted camera so that viewers could watch the events unfold from his own perspective, as if watching someone play the popular first-person shooter games featured on the service.[1]

Gendron's murderous ethnonationalism was based on the "Great Replacement" conspiracy theory, according to which a global Jewish cabal plots to commit "white genocide" by eliminating white-skinned people from Western countries. In this theory, the cabal manipulates governments from behind the scenes to carry out its agenda through permissive policies on issues like immigration and reproductive rights. It sows unrest by using the educational system and the news media to exaggerate racist and gender-related forms of oppression, reinforced through pop culture products like movies, games, and television shows. In perhaps their most nefarious scheme, the conspirators aim to undermine the traditional family unit by pushing non-traditional definitions of gender identity onto the population. The theory is not concerned with the question of why the cabal is doing this, because it needn't be: as an antisemitic ideology, it casts Jewish people as naturally evil, so it requires no further explanation for their motives. Far from some fringe tendency, the "Great Replacement" is a basic conservative talking point regularly echoed on wildly popular prime time news shows like *Tucker Carlson Tonight*.[2]

In the reactionary mind, the globalist agenda goes by various names, sometimes as "Cultural Marxism," or sometimes just "leftism"—the freakout around the amorphous notion of "wokeness" is the most recent version of it. But whatever its form, its function for its adherents is to reconcile certain contradictory facts, like crushing inequality in what is supposed to be the world's premier democracy, or declining living standards in the richest country in history, in a larger narrative that pins the blame for these problems on an evil global elite and its domestic henchmen. By its nature, conspiracy thinking obscures the background of economic and political power that determines our lives so that the miseries it causes can be blamed on various visible figures in the foreground. If one lacks the vocabulary to understand the basic conditions of one's existence, then the anger and fear generated by those conditions will naturally encourage a search for scapegoats to blame for them. This is the source of the enduring hold of conspiracism on the popular imagination, and its stunning growth over the past decade. It is not so much an individual psychological habit as a shared social mood in which people try to make sense of a nonsensical world. Far from confirming the rightwing fantasy of an all-controlling elite, the dramatic rise of mass conspiracism is precisely the opposite: a trend inversely correlated with the declining ability of governments, and the corporate overlords they serve, to exert control over the society they rule. As the collective convulsion of a society coming undone, its continued growth is assured.

This book is about the closure of an era of world history. Perhaps you could call it a kind of epitaph. Over the span of about three generations, from the conclusion of the Second World War to around the mid-2010s, the world economy was characterized by deepening integration: commercial integration, as most nations steadily increased their trade relations with each other, and—particularly after the end of the Cold War—productive integration, as corporations freely invested in or collaborated with companies in other countries to make their products. Corporate and bureaucratic elites in most nations assumed that the world economy would continue to grow at a healthy clip, allowing low- and mid-income countries to catch up with and eventually join the exclusive club of advanced economies in the Global North, namely Europe, North America, and Japan. They also tended to assume that the existing international political order, led and sponsored by the United States after it emerged as the world's undisputed superpower in the 1990s, would persist indefinitely, ensuring a stable environment for international business. The cosmopolitan ideal of a global civilization sailing fitfully but steadily into the future was a leitmotif of the period christened by a million forgotten thinkpieces as the era of "globalization."

The world of that era is now disintegrating, beset by twin plagues of war and pestilence. The COVID-19 pandemic and the re-emergence of European war poured fuel on a fire that was already burning well before them. Instead of growing to incorporate ever more of the world's nations into it, a slowing world economy pits them against each other to fight over the remaining sources of growth; the assumption that low- and middle-income countries can develop to the level of the advanced economies is replaced by the conviction that some countries should be explicitly prevented from doing so; and instead of promoting the cherished ideals and institutions of "free trade," the U.S. government—their former champion—tears them down with hyper-nationalist trade policies that, not so long ago, politicians and economists would have decried as dire violations of the integrity of free markets. Now, bereft of any other ideas, they mostly just nod along with whatever the government is doing.

In fact, the global process of disintegration shows up in the spreading appeal of economic nationalism. Most governments, apparently without much of a choice, are adopting a broadly similar approach of expanding their presence in the national economy while undercutting their rivals in a desperate bid to raise their rates of growth. Yet as I will discuss in some detail in the chapters to follow, national policies are unable to address the source of the problem, which is the secular slowdown in the rate of growth of the *transnational* world economy as a whole. When the rate of growth of the world economy slows, economic competition becomes a more existential, zero-sum affair, as growth for some can only come at the expense of others. In these conditions, nationalist economic policies can temporarily benefit an individual country, but only by undercutting the terms of trade and prospects for growth in other countries, exacerbating the global trend of decline that encourages such policies in the first place. This vicious cycle of economic nationalism is now the background of all world politics. No one really knows what the future holds, but it is worth noting that the last time the global economy came apart under the pressures of planetary crisis, the result was three decades of warfare and industrial depression from 1914 to 1945.

Whatever is to come, it is almost certain to be quite weird—probably more so than anyone expects. Every thirty years or so a massive, global economic crisis comes along that shatters the confidence of the establishment and throws the credibility of its experts into question. When the people who are supposed to know turn out to know nothing, anything goes, and ideas usually dismissed as nonsense can gain traction. The last dozen or so years constitutes such a period. Sheer weirdness enjoys a newfound premium among audiences hungry for answers as their bewildered rulers look on agape, dumbstruck by the results of their own incompetence.

In the classic 1999 science-fiction film *The Matrix*, the protagonist Neo takes the red pill to learn the truth, which is that he lives in a simulation controlled by sentient machines who have enslaved the human race and turned them into a source of energy. "Taking the red pill" has since become a shorthand expression to describe the belief that the media spectacles of politics and entertainment are all an elaborate hoax perpetrated by evil, supernatural, or superterrestrial forces to keep us enslaved, as in *The Matrix*. The protean QAnon movement is a colorful example. Lurid tales about the satanic, child-sacrificing pedophiles who allegedly run the world proliferate like wildfire on social media, while improbable hero figures emerge from the national past. John F. Kennedy, Jr., a hero of QAnon mythology, is expected to return as a messiah to smite the usurpers and deliver the country from evil in an apocalyptic event known as "The Storm." Many participants in the mob who trashed the u.s. Capitol on January 6, 2021, were red-pilled QAnon believers. "Touch your nose if jfk Jr is still alive," one QAnon internet sleuth asked Robert Kennedy, Jr., in a live Instagram chat, who then did proceed to touch his nose.[3] If the choice is between participating in a great patriotic awakening to save the nation, or the boring drone of talking heads on msnbc or cnn, is it any surprise that the red pill is so popular? It does not help, of course, that billionaires and their sycophants are indeed often sexual predators whose lascivious behavior is well documented. The late Jeffrey Epstein, for example, a convicted sex criminal and human trafficker, personally consorted with many of the most powerful people in the world for decades. This does not boost their standing among the general populace.

Far from a purely American curiosity, QAnon is a fully global movement, having sprouted up in over seventy countries.[4] Its international popularity exploded as alarm spread during the covid-19 pandemic about the "Great Reset," the official theme of the 2020 World Economic Forum in Davos, Switzerland. For the QAnon and Q-affiliated community, this was the global elite's grand scheme to abolish private property, institute a communist world government, cull the world population with covid-19, and enslave the rest of humanity with vaccines. But the "Great Reset" is really something far more banal: a proposal by billionaires for international governance based on "stakeholder capitalism," or the notion that governments should work more closely with private businesses to serve not just their shareholders, but society more generally. In practice, of course, "working more closely" with multinational corporations means giving them *more* sway in decision-making processes, more influence in shaping policy outcomes. It means promoting corporate interests to be the main stakeholders in public policy, with government in a secondary position and civil society a mere afterthought, if it matters at all.[5] In other words, the "Great Reset" is anything but what the name suggests; it is more like a public relations campaign for continuing corporate rule, for continuing to allow private corporations to go on pillaging and polluting the world as they have always done.

This book lays out the anatomy of corporate domination, otherwise known as capitalism, and its history to explain how the world has arrived at its present state. Though sometimes focusing on the United States due to its importance within that regime, this is a global story, one shaped not just by the self-aggrandizing billionaires of the Davos crowd, but by the everyday battles conducted by ordinary people of every country against capitalism, not in the fantastical realm of Facebook groups and chain emails but in the world of workplaces, neighborhoods, and city streets. Despite the nationalist turn, the transnational terrain of class and conflict continues to shape the world economy, and a clear sight of these dynamics—the politics and economics of global disintegration—is a basic condition for any effective opposition. But every story must begin somewhere. A global history of the present can illuminate how we got here by beginning with the emergence and untimely demise of the idea formerly known as "globalization."

one

Globalization and Its Double

"The defining document of the globalization system is the Deal."
—THOMAS L. FRIEDMAN[1]

"Deals are my art form."
—DONALD TRUMP[2]

I magine a world in which the inherited divisions between people have become irrelevant. All the old conflicts fueled by war, violence, ideology—the bloody nightmare of history—dissolve into a pacified global landscape of fluid commerce and collaboration. Nations trade with one another on equal terms, with no unfair advantages, because everyone participates in the same global marketplace where competition rewards the best ideas. Universal access to revolutionary communication technologies grants unprecedented freedom of expression to ordinary people the world over who, for the first time in history, have the entire range of human knowledge at their fingertips. Information becomes an abundant resource. And, most importantly, people move with ease across national borders, coming and going as they please in search of the most promising prospects for their work and their lives.

Sound enticing? A certain Thomas Loren Friedman certainly thought so. Friedman, the internationally best-selling author, three-time Pulitzer Prize winner, and renowned sage of the *New York Times* opinion page preached for years the gospel of "globalization." That is, the thesis that the global triumph of liberal democracy, technological breakthroughs like the Internet, and the worldwide expansion of business opportunity would eventually render borders practically obsolete. The result would be an even playing field for all, individuals and countries alike, who for the first time would be fully integrated into a world market where everyone competes on an equal footing and every idea gets its hearing. Borders would not disappear overnight, to be sure, but they would gradually wither away under the twin pressures of interconnection and innovation, as governments the world over were compelled to adopt the same articles of faith to stay competitive: "free trade" and "democracy." Free trade encouraged democratization, and democracies naturally tended toward liberalized trade policies. "The historical debate is over," quipped the guru of globalization in 1999. "The answer is free market capitalism."[3]

It was an age of optimism. For more than a decade and a half from the early 1990s through the mid-2000s, bien-pensant Western elites took for granted the notion of globalization as an irresistible force destined to lead the world toward a harmonious state of responsible liberal governance, enlightened economic management, and the freedom of the market. If even the "post-socialist" states of the former Soviet bloc were adopting these tenets as their own, which they did at a quickening pace in the halcyon days after 1989, then who could seriously doubt it?

Plenty of academics jumped aboard the hype train. After the end of the ideological conflicts of the Cold War, it seemed as if the conditions were coming together for democratic societies to flourish as never before. Paralleling the excitement around the information economy in the business press, cultural critics wrote about the egalitarian implications of digital media, which were ushering in a "control revolution" in which "the Internet is putting individuals in charge and changing the world we know," as proclaimed in the title of a 1999 book by the journalist Andrew Shapiro.[4] Hopeful political scientists and philosophers foresaw an age of democratic renewal based on the greater transparency and accountability that new media would bring to civic life. People would be given an unprecedented capacity to supervise the processes of government, becoming "monitorial citizens," in the historian Michael Schudson's term. Due largely to the efforts of the German philosopher Jürgen Habermas, "deliberative democracy" would become an entire sub-field of research across philosophy, political science, and media studies. The sociologist Manuel Castells prophesied that "The material foundations of society, space, and time are being transformed, organized around the space of flows and timeless time . . . It is the beginning of a new existence, and indeed the beginning of a new age, the Information Age."[5] In perhaps his most famous metaphor, Friedman himself captured the essence of the era in his 2005 international best-seller *The World Is Flat*. Dazzled by the shining vistas of possibility opened up by task management software, he and his fellow flat-earthers in the government, academia, and the pundit pep squad enjoined their peers to get with the program, because this future was imminent—it was only a question of who would most successfully take advantage of it. The flattening of the earth before the onslaught of globalization looked inescapable.

Since Friedman's manifesto was published, the flat-earth doctrine has gained a surprising following of devoted adherents beyond—or, more accurately, below—its initial base in the right-thinking intelligentsia. Only, these believers uphold a more literalist interpretation. The Flat Earth Society maintains that the world is indeed physically flat, not spherical. A consummate product of the "Information Age," its prolific online creators work mainly through networked platforms like YouTube and Facebook to address a rapidly growing community of hundreds of thousands of followers, reaching millions with their content.

Marshaling an impressive range of evidence, flat-earthers can easily dismiss the "scientific fact" of a round earth not only by claiming to disprove it, but more importantly by offering a compelling alternative narrative that makes sense of the world: the round earth consensus is part of a greater campaign of lies by which a global elite manipulates the masses, keeping them in the dark about the true power structure that controls their lives. This narrative provides answers and meaning in a social order that largely provides neither.

The movement has held major conventions in the United States, the United Kingdom, Brazil, and Italy, with more in the works. Its popularity, and apparently its plausibility, are growing.[6] And, unlike their forerunners in the heyday of the globalization hype, these flat-earthers are authentically bottom-up, a grassroots movement spreading their revelation to the people. Sigmund Freud maintained that an encounter with one's double is always, at some level, a meeting with an "uncanny harbinger of death."[7] Born of the very technologies of connection glorified by Friedman, the thriving Flat Earth Society is the uncanny double of yesteryear's flat world movement, a death knell for whatever plausibility the globalization story had left.

The Flat Earth Society is only an especially colorful example of a widespread crisis of legitimacy confronting traditional elites in the wake of the end of globalization as a political and economic project. The end of the Cold War and the collapse of the Soviet Union were supposed to herald a new era of democracy, an enlightened, cosmopolitan order buttressed by expanding world trade, market-friendly economics, and the open, newly abundant flow of information through the fiber optic cables that would soon connect the whole world. Now, and virtually everywhere, a flourishing counter-enlightenment brushes these notions aside as empty bromides, or as nothing more than a mendacious shell game proffered by a corrupt cabal of elites in which ordinary people always lose. Instead of aspirations to accede to a promising new world community, a growing number of people demand to secede from it. From global integration to fragmenting disintegration: this captures the current trajectory of the world.

Drift

Reading the classic literature from the heyday of globalization today makes one smile. Much of it comes off as unintended self-parody, or as soft dystopian fiction.[8] From the start, there was a healthy dose of fantasy motivating the elite consensus, which never had anything like broad-based consent among the general public. Nevertheless, that does not suffice to explain why history turned out so differently from what so many "experts" had predicted. It is worth reflecting for a moment on how strange this all is. For decades scholars, pundits, and politicians alike hailed the growing obsolescence of national barriers, based on the equally inexorable growth of a competitive world market within the "rules-based international order." Philosophers wrote about "the end of history" and the "post-national constellation"; economists deigned to explain to the benighted masses that resistance to the free market was futile, its dictates as unavoidable as natural laws; political leaders intoned the irresistible force of the technological revolution that ignores national traditions and would end class conflict; overpaid pundits proclaimed the advent of a "post-American world" and the supposed "rise of the rest" in a newly leveled international playing field.[9] Respectable opinion makers were certain about a post-national future for humanity as a whole. Now, they tell us with equal certainty about the enduring necessity of the nation-state to secure the existence of separate, unique national communities, indeed for the very survival of democracy.[10]

As it was, liberal homilies foretelling a steady voyage into a world of rising living standards for all, respect for human rights, and international harmony crashed on the hard shoals of extreme inequality, ideological polarization, and the untimely return of geopolitics. This unforeseen turn of events has left the liberal elite—a cohort of educated professionals at the institutional nexus of government, the media, and academia—scrambling to make sense of the world, without any compelling answers for the most important questions of the moment. Their prestige dissipated, their credibility shattered, they are just as confused as the downwardly mobile people they are supposedly qualified to rule, a growing number of whom hold them in seething contempt. The promises of globalization lie in ruins, its victims in worldwide revolt.

The aftermath of this dramatic failure casts its shadow across our entire era. There is no shortage of morbid symptoms expressing the slow, agonizing death of globalization as we knew it, but the recrudescence of ethnicist and nationalist mass movements is the most telling. Across the ideological spectrum, in country after country, forms of political thought and discourse asserting the primacy of the national community as the vehicle of democracy against the invidious forces of globalization are growing in power, in some cases challenging the foundations of political liberalism. Taken by many after the events of 1989 to be the teleological endpoint of human history, liberal democracy now finds its very existence thrown into question, a casualty of the slow-motion disintegration of the global economic system.

In a predictable twist, liberals themselves have emerged as some of the most virulent neo-nationalists. Having given up the old litany of the "third way," which preached a pragmatic mix of unfettered free trade, adroit technical management of the economy, and responsible but minimal social safety nets, they now turn upon it like ex-cultists denouncing their former dogma, issuing a clarion call for a return to national social democracy, or even "strong nationalism," in some cases.[11] Liberal nationalism now directs much of its energy to raging against the external

enemy du jour, whomever it may be. In the United States, for
instance, this movement is clearly visible in the transition over
the last decade from an abstract, stateless official enemy—
"terrorism"—to *powerful states* as the national enemies: Russia,
China, Iran. In the new posture of open confrontation, the u.s.
government is willing fully to weaponize the global monetary
system built around its own currency, the dollar, abolishing the
already flimsy pretext that the system serves as a fair forum for
world trade. While the extreme sanctions leveled against the
Russian economy following the invasion of Ukraine are the most
dramatic example of this, the trend toward weaponization was
already well established in the u.s. elite's implacable hostility to
China, a bipartisan consensus to do whatever it takes to strangle
that country's continued development by leveraging sanctions to
shut it out of foreign markets and block access to key technology.
Plainly subordinating the dollar-based world economy to
geopolitical objectives, the United States has made it crystal clear
that the so-called international community is a euphemism for
the u.s.-dominated global order. In shifting its attention from the
"war on terror" to the confrontation with great power rivals, the
center has gone from upholding the principles of international
trade and cooperation to actively digging their graves.

But the appeal of the new nationalism is pan-ideological.
Among organizers and intellectuals on the left lurks a persistent
belief that bold, large-scale redistributive programs require
globalization to be somehow "rolled back." This common
line of thought implies that some form of disengagement or
"decoupling" from the world market is necessary. It amounts to
a left-wing nationalism based on the blueprint of postwar society,
in which capital, labor, and the state are nominally equal partners
in a power-sharing agreement that forms the basis of social
democracy. Others, such as the Keynesian economist J. W. Mason,
make the full case for decoupling as the road to socialism,
since it is seen as the key condition that must be met to pursue

the ambitious politics of redistribution at the heart of a new socialist movement.[12]

On the far opposite side of the spectrum, one need only point to a ghoulish cast of characters challenging liberal governments or leading far-right regimes of their own: Donald Trump, Boris Johnson, Marine Le Pen, Alexander Gauland, Jair Bolsonaro, Rodrigo Duterte, Viktor Orbán, Matteo Salvini, Vladimir Putin. One could go on. Conservative apologists for these figures share the same notion of class compromise as the social democrats, but dress it up in cringeworthy paeans to the national family, a doctrine known as corporatism which takes its cue from medieval Catholic social thought. Calls for decoupling have recently grown much louder across the political spectrum in the wake of the coronavirus pandemic, which dramatically exposed the fragilities of a world productive system built on supply chains scattered across continents.

It would appear that the project of globalization as we knew it has exhausted itself, and a reassertion of national sovereignty is the only game in town. Despite the appearance of vituperative opposition between left, right, and center, the whole spectrum is drifting toward the same horizon. They are but different inflections of the same core ideology of economic nationalism. Economic nationalists claim that the wealth generated inside a country belongs solely to its legal citizens, and that economic policy should reflect that. It opposes globalism and advocates more domestic control over the economy, locating the essence of democracy in national sovereignty. Steve Bannon, erstwhile advisor to Donald Trump, defines it as a program to "maximize the value of citizenship."[13] Who would disagree with that goal? The intuitive sense of the idea, which is in principle distinguishable from cultural and racialized forms of nationalism, partly explains its pan-ideological appeal. If globalization has been the source of our ills, then the obvious remedy would be to reverse it. Our lives are dominated by gigantic, unaccountable banks and financial institutions—break them up, subject them to national regulation or even public ownership. Tired of the rich escaping taxation by hoarding their wealth in overseas tax havens? Close the loopholes and repatriate it. Ordinary people have been getting pounded for forty years, their standard of living plunging, while the top 10 percent have grown exponentially wealthier, so redistribute the national product with a wealth tax. Out of patience with the corporate oligarchs who rig politics to systematically favor their rules of the game? Buy them out. Have the government purchase all of their financial assets at market prices and convert them into a giant, publicly owned index fund that, as the national economy grows, would pay dividends to the citizenry. All our most debilitating problems seem to stem from our entanglement in an opaque, predatory economic system that is global in scope; naturally, the most ambitious, promising solutions might seem to lie in cutting the cord. Divested from its racist packaging in the addled imagination of the reactionary right, economic nationalism might appear to progressives as the rational ego to the pulsing, nihilistic id of Trumpism.[14]

But this is where the depth of the problem becomes clearer. Economic nationalists can be found of every political stripe, sometimes advocating the same program from what are supposed to be completely opposed positions: the antitrust movement, which seeks to break up large financial institutions in order to introduce more market competition among smaller players, has partisans on both the far right and the far left. While the left is traditionally seen as the guardian of redistribution, seeking to alleviate class inequality through social programs that parcel out the national wealth more fairly, the right now has its own brand of redistributional politics targeting the ultrarich and undocumented foreigners alike. Likewise, closely policed national borders and stricter immigration laws are typically seen as a conservative prerogative, but one also hears pundits making a liberal—or even "leftist"—case for them.[15] Sovereigntism, the movement to reclaim the national state as the only viable terrain of real democracy, comes in left- and rightwing versions—such as "Lexit" vs "Brexit," or the doomed efforts of the Syriza party to liberate Greece from the vice grip of northern European banks. In its tendency to cut across the boundaries of conventional political terms, the principle of economic nationalism is more like a meta-ideology, its premises shared across the spectrum of political opinion as the unquestioned ground underlying its opposing factions. In fact, economic nationalism describes an entire *political economy*, by which I mean the material practices through which a society reproduces itself and the conceptual language in which it apprehends and reflects on that process of reproduction. As such, it has a recurring role across the nineteenth, twentieth, and twenty-first centuries playing the foil to liberal internationalism. More precisely, economic nationalism periodically resurfaces as a counter-political economy to the recurring breakdowns of the modern international order, accompanying it like a shadow from its beginning. To once again invoke the bard of Bethesda, Thomas Friedman: nationalist political economy takes hold in a world that is not flat, but actually "faster, deeper, more fused, open, and fragile," to use one of his pithy re-descriptions of the present.[16]

What Was Globalization?

Looking back at the delirious hype of the 1990s and 2000s, it would be easy to get the impression that globalization had been a radically new, unprecedented phenomenon. That was certainly a widespread perception at the time. In fact, it was nothing of the sort. Grand statements proclaiming a new age of speed, connection, and rapid change are a recurring feature of modernity. At least since the French Revolution, every generation has felt compelled to record its own take on the theme, beginning perhaps most memorably with Marx and Engels' observation in 1848 that the

constant revolutionizing of production, uninterrupted
disturbance of all social conditions, everlasting uncertainty
and agitation distinguish the bourgeois epoch from all
earlier ones. All fixed, fast-frozen relations, with their train
of ancient and venerable prejudices and opinions, are swept
away, all new-formed ones become antiquated before they
can ossify. All that is solid melts into air . . .[17]

In the early twentieth century, it was the telegraph, the steamship,
and the railroad that were the "great cosmic forces," to quote
the sociologist Robert Park, that were breaking down all the
old barriers to usher in a radical new era of connectivity and
cosmopolitanism. Even the postwar era, implicitly seen as
the sleepy precursor of high-speed, late-twentieth century
globalization, was for its contemporaries a time of a "great
world revolution" in which "the rapid spread of literacy, mass
communications, and travel . . . is breaking down traditional
institutions and culture patterns which in the past held societies
together. In short, the world community is becoming both
more interdependent and more fluid than at any other time in
history."[18] The only certainty seems to be that every era seeing
itself as one of rapid connection and change is condemned to
be seen as a period of slow, staid isolation by its successor.

Considering the economic realities of the post-Cold War
moment also quickly deflates the hyperbole of the era. From the
end of the Cold War through the mid-1990s, the average growth
in the international trade of products and services was 4.5 percent
less than during the boom period from 1950 to 1973, and only
marginally higher than in the period from 1853 to 1872. Moreover,
average growth in gross world product over the same period was
just 1 percent, compared to 5.3 percent from 1950 to 1973, and
2.3 percent from 1973 to 1990. Taking gross product per capita as
a measure, the picture is still more underwhelming: from 1990
until 2003, the heyday of post-Cold War globalization, U.S. GDP

growth per capita was a mere 1.74 percent, considerably less than the 2.45 percent of the postwar period, and less even than the crisis-ridden decade and a half from 1973 to 1990 (1.96 percent), a period afflicted by severe inflation and deep economic depression. Over the same period, the world economy in general expanded at a modestly faster clip of 1.81 percent, still a far smaller rate of growth than from 1950 until 1973 (2.92 percent), despite the world-historical integration of enormous new markets in China and India.[19] These data indicate that all the celebrations of speed, connectivity, and openness during the heyday of globalization should be understood relative to the overall *stagnation* of the world economy, not to some dizzying expansion. In its injunction that people everywhere must adjust to the supposedly new realities of a hyper-connected world, globalization talk worked as an ideological discourse, propagating the notion that, since there is no alternative, everyone must become more creative, more productive, more valuable to survive. The competitive mood of the discourse reflected the decreasing vitality of the private economy, and the resulting sense of tightening competition this creates for those who own that economy. In a society where the economy is privately controlled, like ours, the neuroses of its owners tend to spread throughout society at large via the influence they exert over political and media institutions.

Yet even if the breathless hype around globalization was more mystification than substance, it does not mean the concept is entirely empty. As a shorthand for the formation of a global economy through accelerating traffic in commodities, people, and ideas, "globalization" names the expansionary dynamic at the heart of the modern world. Starting by most accounts with the advent of scientific industrialism in the late eighteenth century, but with roots running back to the seventeenth and sixteenth centuries, the thickening ties of commerce and communication have gradually, if unevenly, brought most of the planet's inhabitants into closer contact with one another. Despite the regular interruptions of war and economic crisis, the overall trend for several centuries has been toward a world-spanning network of markets through which all (or almost all) of its countries are economically integrated. This is the process by which the "globe" in globalization was wrought.

The Scottish philosopher Adam Smith gave perhaps the most influential theory of this process. In his *Inquiry Into the Nature and Causes of the Wealth of Nations*, Smith maps it out as a free creation of human reason: an innate, natural propensity in individuals to "truck, barter, and trade" leads to the spontaneous emergence of markets, integrated networks for exchanging commodities. At the same time, the extension of such markets and the reorganization of the economy along their lines eventually ignites the transformative force of the division of labor, which is for Smith the motor of human history. The division of labor, in its turn, brings growing productivity and the possibility of increasing returns on investment, generating revenues as profits, rents, and wages for an expanding pool of people. This then opens up new markets, and so the benign process continues. Smith christened the whole cycle, along with its political expression in individual property rights and the rule of law, the "System of Natural Liberty."

As the gospel of globalization has it, the system of free trade will eventually allow all countries steadily to raise their standard of living and converge toward peaceful coexistence amid rising, shared prosperity. This is the classic narrative of liberal cosmopolitanism, the ideal of a self-sustaining order of individual liberty buttressed by the natural laws of the market. The cosmopolitan narrative sees the equity inherent in the market as the core of civil society, a free domain opposite the state and constituted through the voluntary commercial activity of individuals bounded by contractual law. It knows not collective identity, nor the borders of national governments; its fundamental actor is the individual as a self-interested monad, its most elemental institution the market. Its setting, implicitly, is the whole world as an aggregate of particular commodity traders, whose unforced transactions with one another propel the engine of civilizational progress. This progressive sense of history motivated by the rights of the market defines the identity of the social class formerly known as the bourgeoisie, the owners of society's means of production. Through the providence of the market's invisible hand, Smith's famous metaphor, the bourgeois pursuit of private commercial gain would create general prosperity, as more markets meant more opportunities for investment, and more investment meant rising incomes for all.

A reassuring story, imbued with the aura of science through the mental toil of generations of economists. Yet from the start the cosmopolitan tale was contradicted by a counter-narrative that criticized the unrealistic assumptions beneath its atomistic worldview. Economic nationalism seizes upon the political power of the nation state as the means to realize the moral fables of liberalism in the face of the latter's own failure to secure them. As such, it constitutes a kind of intrinsic critique of liberalism. For open participation in the world market, it substitutes the growth and welfare of the collective community, always stressing a fundamental theme: the need to protect "our" economy, assets, or property from unfair competition or foreign ownership. Instead of civil society and the market, it emphasizes the state as the guarantor of economic freedom; instead of "free trade," it calls for protectionism; and, maybe most crucially, it imposes limits on the free circulation of money capital, that is, finance, in the name of national sovereignty, the political right to self-determination. These policy objectives are different chords in the same liberal key of "fairness," or parity, the claim to what rightfully belongs to "us." Like liberal cosmopolitanism, economic nationalism rests on an unquestioned, presumed institutional basis of money and property ownership.

But importantly, it is an "us," rather than a "me." Economic nationalism denies the major premise of liberal cosmopolitanism, the calculating, utilitarian individual as the basic unit of economic life, and substitutes the nation state in its place. From this standpoint, the idea of a secular trend toward rising, common prosperity based on the gradual spread of free trade to the benefit of all is revealed to be a fiction, as it ignores the fact that nation-states exist, and, further, that they exist in an unequal competitive struggle with one another. This oversight blinds laissez-faire liberalism to the chief consequence of its own vision: economic competition in a fully open world market leads not to universal prosperity for all, but instead to the prosperity of some and the ruin of others. The only way to remedy this outcome is for governments themselves to become the engineers of economic policy, structuring markets for the maximum benefit of their population through a proactive fiscal policy and protectionist measures like tariffs, capital controls, and subsidies. Pursued not in accord with other countries, but at their expense, the principal aim is to raise productivity and competitiveness, particularly by expanding the manufacturing sector, through a state-driven industrial policy. With its origins in the dawn of the nineteenth century, the political economy of nationalism arises to oppose the international order of the world market, in which the market primarily mediates competition between private firms, and replaces it with explicit competition between countries, that is, between nations acting as giant firms. But it does so from within the same liberal worldview that takes the categories of property ownership, the rule of law, and individual rights as self-evident truths, simply seeing a more proactive government as the practical means to make them a reality.

As a distinct political economy, nationalism is close but not identical to the realm of economic statecraft known as mercantilism. Mercantilist policies aim to strengthen the competitive position of the state in the world market through the domestic development of key strategic industries. They typically reject the doctrine of free trade as a convenient fiction that masks the naked self-interest of the currently dominant economic power, which, in however a fashion, stands to benefit the most from laissez-faire policies in other countries. This stance frees the visible hand of the state to actively shape its economy. Historically, mercantilist regimes have usually pursued a positive balance of trade by closely managing the technological modernization of domestic industries so that they may compete effectively in the world market. While different kinds of states pursue mercantilist trade strategies for different reasons, a strong defense and the ability to project military force through modernized industry are frequently chief among them. But whatever form it takes, mercantilism aims at the empowerment of the state itself relative to its competitors. Thus its attraction for pre-national, imperial modernizers, such as Egypt's Muhammad Ali in the early nineteenth century, or the modernizing radicals of the Japanese government during the Meiji Restoration.[20] It also has characterized sub-national units, such as the Venetian Republic, whose government actively cultivated export industries like luxury textiles to support its hegemony over Mediterranean trade during the fourteenth and fifteenth centuries. For regimes like these, augmenting the economic and military power of the state to prepare it for imperial competition over territory and markets is by far the most important objective of mercantilist trade policy, while the welfare and rights of the population are a distant second, if they count at all.

By contrast, economic nationalism stresses the specifically *national* aspect of development, the cultural, moral, productive evolution of a distinct people.[21] As a philosophy and practice, it has a liberal temper, aiming at the empowerment of some community of feeling, heritage, blood, or tradition—of some idealized civil society, however conceived. It is predicated on the separation of state and society, public and private, government and market, taking state power as an instrument to serve the national interest. All forms of nationalism are based on the fundamentally modern idea of self-determination. It may involve territorial ambitions, but the core of the national concept is an inherently unique group of people moving together through time into an open future, forging its collective fate as one. If the logic of mercantilism is spatial, the logic of economic nationalism is temporal, based on the internal development and destiny of the national community. And all imperial mercantilist regimes, without exception, have eventually become organized as nation states, the universal political unit of the modern world order.

Economic nationalism is thus the twin of globalization, having never been absent from its history. This should not be surprising: if increasing economic interconnectivity is a defining feature of the modern world, so is its political division into competing nation states. This basic condition, taken as a sheer, inexplicable fact, is the setting for the classic articulation of economic nationalist philosophy in Friedrich List's *The National System of Political Economy*. List was a vigorous German nationalist active in the political and economic reconstruction of Europe in the wake of the Napoleonic Wars. To him, writing in the first great age of national awakening, the nation-state appeared to be just as ontologically basic to human existence as the market did to Adam Smith: both are expressions of the "laws of logic and the nature of things," to use List's phrase. "History is there to prove that protective regulations originated either in the natural efforts of nations to attain to prosperity, independence, and power, or in consequence of wars and of the hostile commercial legislation of predominating manufacturing nations," List avers in his quarrel with the classical school of political economy.

> The idea of independence and power originates in the very idea of "the nation." The school never takes this into consideration, because it does not make the economy of the separate nation, but the economy of society generally, i.e. of the whole human race, the object of its investigations.[22]

The cosmopolitan ideal of universal prosperity, if it is possible, could only be realized through the administrative oversight of particular states with particular interests of their own. It is the logic of the market projected onto nation states: from the interaction of many particular interests, general harmony—somehow—will emerge.

List is notable for articulating the economic philosophy of nationhood in what is perhaps its most strikingly clear formulation, displaying its contradictions in their purest form. At its base is an unquestioned, metaphysical presumption: since nation states exist, so will they always. All the conclusions of political economy, for List as for any economic nationalist, are functions of this inert, given fact. This presumption is the converse of the narrative lauding globalization as an inevitable, natural force—only making the nation state, rather than the market, into a permanent, unalterable feature of reality. The cosmopolitan liberal order of peaceful co-development can be preserved, but only if the great economic powers can aggressively pursue their self-interest at the expense of their competitors, regardless of the consequences. If this incoherent notion sounds familiar, it is because economic nationalism has once again become fashionable today as the cure for chronically ill national economies.

Global history in the modern age swings between these two ideological poles like a pendulum. At times, the international mechanisms of the market are broadly taken to be the ultimate arbiters of the fate of nations, from which there is no appeal—as in the high tide of neoliberalism. At other times, it is widely assumed to be self-evident that national governments must take an active hand in maximizing the economic welfare of their populations in the absence of any automatic trend toward greater prosperity—the creed of both social democracy and national conservatism. In these periods, the nation state is the privileged side of the same basic dualism. As in List's time, so today the pious encomiums to the virtues of free markets and liberal trade of yesterday are quickly forgotten, replaced by a new statism in which both liberals and conservatives, a neo-mercantilist center and the nativist right converge on an invigorated nationalism to revive their sputtering economies. Just as the only relevant question for Thomas Friedman's contemporaries as they faced the supposed obsolescence of the nation state was "what kind of global citizen will you be?," the only relevant question for today's thought leaders, facing the obsolescence of globalization, is "what kind of nationalist will you be?" Of course, the more important question of *why* it turned out this way is almost never broached.

Oscillations

The philosopher Hegel, in a well-known quip, said that "the owl of Minerva only takes flight with the coming nightfall."[23] His point is that the true meaning of events only becomes available to us retrospectively. The owl, that is, knowledge, only begins to fly when the day is done, once we can look back at the way things actually turned out to see how it diverged from what people expected, from what they thought they knew. Hence the first step to understanding the present is to grasp it as a concrete historical outcome. Looking at it as the culmination of a certain process will help us to see the parameters of what is possible and what is necessary in the contemporary moment. A brief survey of the key turning points in the world economy from the last century and a half can therefore illuminate the present as history—more precisely: as a result of the *global* history of the modern world.

As a distinct field of inquiry, global history looks beyond the individual nation, region, or civilization to analyze how these units are constituted through interconnection with each other. This means not only describing how they are interdependent, but grasping the form such dependence takes, and crucially, how such forms are imagined and understood by historical contemporaries.

Forms of integration explain how different societies can participate in the same larger, structural context at the same time yet experience it in different ways. Integration can have technological, economic, cultural, or even biological dimensions, and it can occur at the regional, continental, or planetary scale, but its most important aspect is that it transforms over time. Global history, as the historian Sebastian Conrad defines it, "pursues the question of causality up to the global level."[24]

As a systemic analysis of social life at this level, political economy provides concepts for treating causality at a global scale. Surveying history from this elevated height, one can make out certain generational shifts in the overall pattern of economic relationships, along with the ways these relationships are imagined. This history, punctuated by structural transformations in the world economy, traces the transnational outline of *capital*. This is capital not in its conventional economic definition as a factor of production, or as the cost of inputs to produce a certain output. Rather, it denotes a form of integration, a specific way of organizing material life that binds the various world economies together into an interdependent whole greater than the sum of its parts. This whole undergoes structural transformation over time. Responses of different societies to the global problems this presents then, in turn, further influence and impact the evolution of that larger context, a process of historical feedback whose effects define the arc of modern history. The specific problem of growth, which touches nearly all aspects of life in capitalist societies, makes much of politics into a perpetual attempt to manage the process of integration in a crisis-ridden capitalist world system.

As discussed above, the liberal worldview sees economic growth as a felicitous, quasi-natural fact. Whether growth is mediated through supply and demand (the market) or an activist government (the state), modern societies simply grow, trade expands, people get richer. As incomes increase, living standards improve. Self-evidently, the economist points out, growth is a good thing, so we should focus our attention on the conditions that best support it. Open markets, the rule of law protecting the private ownership of property, the free movement of money and commodities, the profit motive as a reward for taking risks—factors like these set the stage for entrepreneurial initiative, the heart of capitalist economies. But all this addresses the question of "how?," instead of "why?," ignoring the inherent weirdness of the notion of unending expansion. After all, why should societies expect to grow endlessly? Why is perpetual growth necessary? For that matter, what exactly is "economic growth" anyway? And why must it take the form that it does, that is, the constant, restless accumulation of commodities, of ever more products and services sold for money? What is the point? Putting these questions to the average economist would be like asking a priest of ancient Sumer why the god Enlil controls the fertility of the land. After a puzzled look, the priest would likely respond that he simply does, and the important thing is to do whatever is necessary to appease him so that the harvest will be abundant. For us moderns, it is above all else the gods of growth who must be satisfied.

But taking these questions seriously means putting aside the theological niceties of academic economics. The expansionary dynamic of modern society, its specific form of growth, and the institutions that support it are actually rooted in historically unique social arrangements, though they are presupposed as natural in economic thought and the liberal political theory built upon it. Since the early nineteenth century, the majority of humanity has been gradually drawn into the orbit of a world market whose tempo sets the rhythm and molds the substance of their working lives, pressing it into the same basic form everywhere. In this form, the primary purpose of labor becomes not to produce one's own means of subsistence, nor to produce things or services that are directly useful to society, but rather to produce a money surplus for the business one works for. In this class-based system, useful goods are produced, of course, but whether or not they get produced is secondary to the deeper need to turn a profit. No profit, no investment, no work.

The owner, then, is compelled to grow his surplus by reinvesting it anew to produce a greater return. This is capital: the cycle of investment, profit, and reinvestment on an expanding basis. Note the contradictory nature of this arrangement: the material and psychological needs of people—those whose work produces the profits—are subordinated to the capitalist's need for growth no matter what, to the constant need for more profits, regardless of the cost to human health, culture, or the natural environment. The more human and ecological needs are sacrificed to the gods of growth, the more unstable society becomes, and the more the unconditional drive for profit undermines the conditions for profit-making. At the same time, society depends on the cycle of capital to provide employment, income, and resources—in short, to materially reproduce itself. When the cycle slows, society breaks down and begins to disintegrate. The result is an inherently chaotic form of economic life constantly beset by crisis. Nevertheless, the general organization of work for the production and reinvestment of capital, its accumulation, is the internal engine of the world market. Because the basic premise of capital is growth without end, so the market must expand without limit until it covers every corner of the planet.

Until the early twentieth century, the industrializing countries and their colonial peripheries had been joined, for several generations, in a world-spanning economic order defined by extensive cross-border flows in people, money, and commodities. The classical era of liberal capitalism, sometimes periodized from 1789 to 1914 as the "long nineteenth century," was widely imagined by its bourgeois rulers to be moving firmly on the tracks of historical progress.[25] Despite occasional setbacks, the story went, science, industry, and the natural, self-regulating laws of the market would work in tandem to spread the benefits of modern civilization to everyone. Progress was inevitable. The historic confidence of the bourgeoisie in this period was evocatively captured in the great World's Fairs of the nineteenth century's second half—massive, sprawling spectacles embodying the ideology of progress in their exhibitions showing off the many scientific and technological achievements of the era.

Yet because of the huge scale of concentrated investment required by industrial capitalism, the great powers—mainly the United Kingdom, the United States, France, Germany, and Japan—eventually sought to boost the profitability of their corporations by seeking out new markets with cheaper materials and labor abroad. Their imperialist adventures usually involved the savage subjugation of local populations in South and East Asia, Africa, and the South Pacific through military conquest, so that they could be organized as an exploitable workforce whose products could be cheaply imported by the home country, and whose wages could then buy exports from it. Imperial apologists blessed all of it as a "civilizing mission" that would carry the benefits of bourgeois society to the backward peoples of the colonial territories. Then as now, imperialism was cast as the other side of civilizational progress. Some version of the progress narrative was the common ideological currency of all the industrializing countries which, regardless of their local political complexion or form of government—liberal or traditionalist, republic or monarchy—were all compelled to adopt the same political economy of manufacturing-led heavy industry, liberalized trade, and exclusive access to overseas markets through imperial possessions. To use lingo today's punditocracy would readily understand, this was "Globalization 1.0."

Of course, as the word implies, this international civilization was an assemblage of individual nations. Eventually, the centrifugal forces of nationalism would rip this first iteration of global capitalist society apart. As industrial depression enveloped the advanced economies toward the turn of the nineteenth century, strengthening protectionism stimulated the emergence of a complementary reaction formation: a belief in the unique, singular identity of each "people," which essentially distinguishes it from all others. As governments disregarded the nostrums of free trade in favor of more aggressively protectionist measures, unavoidable in a tightly competitive world market, and so dismantled the ties of economic dependency in the pursuit of nationalist economics, so they stoked the embers of nationalist reaction. The story of progress, much like today, began to look more like a descent into a uniquely modern barbarism. By 1914, those embers erupted into a firestorm that engulfed the capitalist world.

In the long sequence of planetary conflict and depression lasting from the First World War to the end of the Second World War, classical liberal capitalism disintegrated into a maelstrom of fire and blood. In the wake of two rounds of total war on a global scale—a period some historians classify as the "Second Thirty-Years War"—bookending the unprecedented economic destruction wrought by the Great Depression, a new political economy emerged, supposedly correcting for the catastrophic failures of its predecessor. During the middle decades of the twentieth century a new consensus came together across the developed—and now also the post-colonial—worlds. Reversing the certainties of the classical liberal period, unregulated markets were now almost unanimously held to be inherently destructive. Now, the way forward for modern societies would lie through semi-planned national economies and the increasingly generous welfare states they provided for—the so-called "mixed economy" combining state planning with regulated private markets. Instead of individualistic competition, popular ideology celebrated a new egalitarianism, centering on the responsibility of governments to provide for the welfare of all their citizens. Elites, for their part, widely believed that the periodic tendency of capitalism to descend into protracted, civilization-threatening crises could be banished through scientific management of the economy. Again, the trend was universal, forming the worldwide basis of legitimacy for the representative democracies of the West, the so-called communist countries of the East, and the state-directed industrial policies of the decolonizing countries. For several generations, it seemed that the "economic problem," as John Maynard Keynes called it, had been solved once and for all.

This too was all an illusion. The state-managed paradigm, in turn, would crash on the shoals of a grinding, inflationary spiral that enveloped the industrial core of the world economy in the 1970s. Its collapse would precipitate another global crisis that eventually, in the 1980s, allowed the resurgence of the nineteenth-century ideals of market supremacy and extreme individualism that all but the most obstinate cranks had thought were the dead artifacts of a more primitive phase of society. The stage was set for a new kind of liberal internationalism—neoliberalism— to be built atop the ruins of state-regulated capitalism. This era, Globalization 2.0, was the world Friedman would so poetically capture.

Fast forward some thirty years or so to the present. Looking back from the current neo-nationalist revival in the twilight of Globalization 2.0, it is clear that global history has been defined, like a pendulum, by dramatic swings between periods of international openness and national closure, both accompanied by general shifts in the tenor of elite thinking and mass ideology. The present nationalist moment, which consciously hearkens back to the mid-century golden age of managed capitalism, is thus a repetition with a difference, just as neoliberalism had been with respect to the first form of globalization. And just as the experts have been certain many times before about the timeless features of a temporary arrangement, so today's consensus around the need to return to the nation state sees it as the only viable option to redeem the undeniable failures of globalization. Society is condemned to an eternal present of never-ending crisis management. As Marx once said, "the fact that the movement of capitalist society is full of contradictions impresses itself most strikingly on the practical bourgeois in the changes of the periodic cycle through which modern industry passes, the summit of which is the general crisis."[26] The crisis beats its lessons into the brains of the ruling class regardless of what they thought they knew.

two

Undertow

The modern English word "crisis" stems from the ancient Greek verb *krinein*, to make a judgement so that a decision may be taken. Its related noun, *krisis*, is the critical moment when one must decide under dangerous or unstable circumstances. In ancient medicine the word had a biological meaning, describing an organism's sickness and subsequent recovery from a pathogenic condition. In medical treatment, the *krisis* came in the course of disease, indicating the turning point in which a patient would either start to recover by the natural healing process, eventually returning to health, or begin to die. Our sense of the word "crisis" today carries this sense of affliction and treatment, of the need to resolve a dangerous deviation from an otherwise healthy or normal situation.

The medical usage of "crisis" parallels its meaning in dramatic art. In classical tragedy, the crisis is the moment of shattering, when characters discover that their fate is governed by a clash of incommensurable truths, of an irresolvable conflict between suprahuman forces played out through the action of the plot. This clash is the undoing of the story's protagonists, unless they can somehow preserve their freedom by casting off the old myths to remake themselves in the image of something new—new laws, new institutions, new myths. The common thread is the critical turning point within a larger process of change, a general calamity that throws human existence into question, but also opens a window of time in which some kind of resolution becomes possible. Recovery, freedom, a different way of living—the new, if it is to come, emerges from this window.

The Italian socialist philosopher and organizer Antonio Gramsci managed to evoke all of these ideas in his well-known description of the crises afflicting capitalist societies. "Sometimes a crisis occurs lasting for decades," he observed while imprisoned by Benito Mussolini's fascist regime in the early 1930s. "The exceptional duration means that incurable structural contradictions have revealed themselves, and that, despite this, the political forces struggling to conserve and defend the existing structure itself are making every effort to cure them, within certain limits, and to overcome them."[1] These are the forces of reaction, which hasten to preserve the traditional hierarchies of a condemned world even as it is falling apart. The reactionary attitude toward crisis is well captured in the famous dictum, "if we want things to stay as they are, things will have to change," spoken by an aristocratic character in *The Leopard*, a classic novel by one of Gramsci's contemporaries, the aristocrat Giuseppe Tomasi di Lampedusa. If socialists believe in the possibility of resolving the impasse into a new social arrangement, one in which the economy would not have to run on a surplus extracted from a subaltern class, then the political right aims to preserve the existing privileges of the powerful in a dying order, whatever it takes. This paradox of experimentation for the sake of preservation, introducing the new to preserve the obsolete, is the key development in rightwing politics across the world over the last decade.

Global Tides

We are currently living through a hiatus like the one Gramsci described. Globalization has failed, yet the social regime it represented—the corporate domination of society at all

levels—remains firmly in place. Facing a popular backlash
and desperate for new strategies of order, political elites have
everywhere returned to notions of the activist state to resecure
their legitimacy, that is, the ideological basis for corporate
absolutism. As a result, one of the most visible symptoms of
the current interregnum is the feverish neo-nationalism that
has overspread the world in the last dozen years or so. The
notion that globalization could be cancelled or rolled back
to some prelapsarian state is the leitmotif of politics across
the 36 countries that make up the Organisation for Economic
Cooperation and Development (OECD). Assuming different
forms in different contexts, the general drift of the world into
a nationalist revival is at this point a fait accompli.

To begin with a demonstrative example, consider the
interminable shitshow known as Brexit in the United Kingdom.
In an outcome unforeseen by the country's Tory government, a
2016 popular referendum on the continuing membership of the
UK in the European Union returned a very slim majority vote
of No. Lauded by both "Brexiteers" on the right and even some
"Lexiteers" on the left, this unexpected result was then turned
into a noble campaign to wrest sovereignty away from scheming
EU bureaucrats and return it to the British people. By repudiating
the technocrats in Brussels, Brexit was to open up a bright new
era of greatness and self-determination for the former imperial
nation. Perhaps it could reopen the door to a renewed, worldwide
Anglosphere of trade zones and defense cooperation, echoing
the days of the Empire. Instead, nearly every macroeconomic
indicator in the country has plummeted dramatically since the
tragicomic spectacle began.[2] Of course, that has not prevented
the country's richest residents from amassing even more wealth
since the referendum took place—a feature, not a bug, for the
Brexiteer right.[3]

Nostalgia for imperial greatness is hardly limited to the
British Isles. British conservatives share the ideal of a restored

imperial dominion with Vladimir Putin, the Russian president, who takes the project of a restored Russosphere seriously enough to have launched a ground invasion of Ukraine aimed at carving out a zone of influence akin to the old Russian Empire. Brexit is mostly a joke while the war in Ukraine is maniacally serious, but both the former UK prime minister, Boris Johnson, and Putin believe in the possibility of a new imperium built on the ruins of globalization.

On the West European continent, an embattled center retains a precarious grip on government, having fought off electoral challenges from the left and right to a stalemate. Governing coalitions led by legacy parties of the center left hold office in Spain and Germany, while the center right governs the Netherlands. France offers an especially clear window into the direction of centrist governments in a post-globalized world. The steady rightward drift of the center is clearly visible in the "Jupiterian" presidency of Emmanuel Macron, a leading figure in calling for strict controls at the European border to halt migration into the EU—a new Fortress Europe for a post-globalized age. Supported by about a quarter of the French population but beloved by establishment pundits the world over, Macron claims to represent neither the traditional left nor the right, but instead an enlightened center, which is in practice a kind of hybrid that fuses neoliberal technocracy with top-down, personalized rule. His emphasis on order, security, and free markets, mixed with a neo-colonial foreign policy, particularly in the Sahel region of West Africa, make him the face of a new, autocratic type of liberalism. After his election to the French presidency in 2017 the former banker declared that "France needs a king," and that such a ruler is necessary to fill the "void" of French democracy.[4] Shortly thereafter his government effectively declared a permanent state of emergency by passing a suite of emergency counter-terrorism powers into law, powers that were soon used to repress popular demonstrations in 2018 and 2019. His party,

Renaissance (formerly La République en Marche!), has introduced legislation to reduce the size of parliament, supposedly to make the government more business-like and closer to the "contractual republic" Macron has invoked as his ideal model.

Severe global inflation has prompted some revisions to this model. For example, Macron has also endorsed "economic planning," saying that the French government will need to take control of key firms in the country's energy sector to strengthen its economic independence.[5] It might seem inconsistent for a regime that postures as a liberal champion of the free market to make noises about the state control of industry, or to militarize border security while extolling the human rights of the individual. In fact, such contradictions reflect the increasingly autocratic, incoherent drift of contemporary liberalism. In this sense, Macron truly is the face of the future.

To the east, the Indian subcontinent has steadily progressed down a path of majoritarian nationalist rage fueled by home-grown religious fanaticism. Emboldened by a prime minister, Narendra Modi, who has deep ties of his own to India's ultraright Hindutva movement, Hindu nationalism has emerged as one of the government's key strategies for maintaining legitimacy in a stalled-out economy where both public and private investment have been declining for over a decade.[6] Virulently xenophobic, Hindutva ideology proclaims the racial superiority of India's traditional Hindu culture to its myriad social and religious minorities, above all to the country's Muslim population. But its hostility is by no means limited to Muslims: Ajit Doval, India's National Security Advisor, has described India as the site of a strategic war between "the People," having given their democratic mandate to the government, and "civil society," defined as artists, intellectuals, activists, virtually anyone critical of Modi's Bharatiya Janata Party (BJP) regime.[7] Facing rising instability from a deteriorating economy, the government stokes conflict between its electoral majority and the rest of the country. One sees a similar pattern of majoritarian chauvinism in Turkey, where the ruling Justice and Development Party, led by Recep Tayyip Erdoğan, casts the political situation as a conflict between its electoral majority and Turkey's internal and external enemies. These enemies are defined as an alliance of domestic dissidents of any kind and foreign financial saboteurs, often explicitly identified as Jewish. Neo-Ottomanism is the watchword in Turkey, as Erdoğan, with his garish, colossal presidential palace in Ankara, militaristic foreign policy, and Islamist culture wars, tries to expand the nation's sphere of influence by conjuring the legacy of that long-dead empire.

Downward trends in global growth have also stoked tensions in East Asia, spilling over into neo-mercantilist rivalry accompanied, as one would expect, by rising national hostility. Under a series of conservative premiers, beginning with the late Abe Shinzo, who see a return to traditional familial and militaristic values as the key to national rebirth, Japan has pursued increasingly aggressive tactics against its regional trade partners in a bid to revive its economy. These have included export bans on certain intermediate goods to South Korea geared toward undermining that country's competitiveness in high-end manufacturing, particularly the all-important semiconductor sector. The bans came after the Korean High Court decided that a major Japanese steel producer, Nippon Steel, should pay a substantial sum to the families of Korean workers conscripted into forced labor under Japan's colonial administration a century ago. Thus the trade war is aggravating simmering tensions between the two countries stemming from the brutal Japanese occupation of the Korean Peninsula in the first half of the twentieth century.

Casting a shadow over the Japan–Korea conflict is the ascent of their giant neighbor to world power status. Under the leadership of Xi Jinping, president of the Republic of China and General Secretary of the Chinese Communist Party, China's government has gradually re-centralized control after several decades of economic and political liberalization following the close of the first Cold War. National harmony at all costs is required to confront the threat of a hostile, belligerent West, the official discourse runs, so that China may secure its historic seat at the global table following the catastrophe known in China as the "century of humiliation," in which the country was carved up at the hands of colonial occupiers and apportioned between them like fiefdoms. Invoking an ethnic sense of national identity rooted in Han Chinese culture, Chinese leadership presents this confrontation as a civilizational clash, like the United States, only in reverse fashion: China stands for equality of opportunity in global development, for the rights of the poor countries to pursue development as they see fit, and for international peace, which the United States is disrupting.[8] The pursuit of peace, as so often, entails modernizing the military and expanding defense spending to prepare for open conflict, preparations taking place, as in the United States, in the context of decelerating growth rates.

Agitated nations, aggressive states, the steady beat of war drums in the distance—these are the themes of a fractured world. The political leadership of virtually every country dreams of restoring greatness based on the ideals and memory of the past; few have anything hopeful or promising to offer for visions of the future. In fact, the future has been all but foreclosed in the addled public discourse of most countries today. There are notable exceptions to this. In China and France, the ideology of modernizing progress into a better future survives at the cost of escalating xenophobia and domestic repression. In Germany, where the governing coalition's motto is "Dare more progress" (*Mehr Fortschritt wagen*), modernization means hitching the prospects for fighting climate change to free market radicalism and a belligerent foreign policy, unprecedented for postwar Germany. In all cases, a forced choice between nostalgic yearning for a lost past and a dystopian parody of progress is the future on offer from neo-nationalism. Originally formulated amid the gathering war clouds of the 1930s, Gramsci's interregnum, replete with morbid symptoms, perfectly describes the world situation today.

American Meltdown

The psychodrama of politics in America is an especially colorful staging of a worldwide trend. The ideological currents swirling around former president Donald Trump, the gameshow host and part-time professional wrestling personality, are a case in point. As is well known, Trumpism hearkens back to a time when America was supposedly great, promising to put national interests first again by opposing the shadowy "globalists" and their chief co-conspirator, China. Overlapping to a great degree with traditional American Christian nationalism, victimization and revenge are its main themes, locating blame for the country's malaise in a demonology featuring China and Jewish financiers like George Soros as lead villains, who in the Trumpist imagination command a variety of henchmen, including Democrats, college professors, public school teachers, immigrants, Antifa, and Black Lives Matter activists, to name just a few. As a worldview, the drama of Trumpism centers on the confrontation between these evil characters and red-blooded American patriots who guard the traditional values of religion, patriarchy, and the bourgeois family. For the true believers this is a millenarian struggle with the demonic on the brink of the end-times. For them, trade conflict is merely a way of prosecuting the spiritual battle, which is the real front of the war.

While the full ideology of Trumpism is confined to a mostly white, Christian minority of the population, the matter is different with its trade and foreign policy narrative, which has since gone fully mainstream. This did not happen easily. During his tenure, Trump himself had become the locus of a bitter conflict between opposing factions of the ruling class, exposing a rift within the U.S. state. His steady emphasis on economic conflict with China, however half-baked, and his derogation of the "ridiculous" leadership of the national security agencies infuriated the entrenched foreign policy and intelligence establishment.[9] His suggestions of a rapprochement with Russian President Vladimir Putin, in particular, were beyond the pale for a faction whose primary responsibility is to maintain the conditions for U.S. global militarism, a crucial pillar of its international power and the lucrative source of fat contracts for the enormous U.S. weapons industry. At the same time, his loyalty to business elites—whom he rewarded with one of the biggest tax cuts in history in 2018—and the promise of new markets and favorable trade deals endeared the bloviating orange man to corporate America. The only problem was Trump himself, who was simply too weird and erratic for the stewards of U.S. empire to keep around.

That problem was soon resolved. Since Trump's exit in 2020, the conflict within the U.S. ruling class has been partially muted, as all parties have reached a new *modus vivendi*. Inveterate hostility to China has solidified into the elite consensus of the U.S. political establishment, bringing Republicans and Democrats, far-right extremists and liberal centrists together in a common cause. Taking the torch from Trump, the Biden administration refashioned the principles of Trumpism into a more recognizably liberal project. The trade conflict begun incompetently under its predecessor has since morphed into an all-out techno-economic war, prosecuted unilaterally by the United States but dressed up as a civilizational struggle between the opposing principles of democracy and autocracy.

The elective affinity between liberal centrists and rightwing extremists for pursuing open conflict with China is rooted in the same anxiety, which is that the United States has become weak, divided, and without a larger sense of purpose. As the überpundit Matthew Yglesias mused in one of his deep thoughts, "anti-China politics could be the unifying national project we need."[10] A glance at the editorial archive of the *Washington Post*, a Jeff Bezos-owned organ of the Democratic Party, and the Rupert Murdoch-owned *Wall Street Journal*, bastion of U.S. conservatism, yields an obsessive rash of articles all calling for the same thing: the need to "beat" China, a goal whose meaning is almost never clarified. Fox News and MSNBC, supposedly polar opposites, speak in one voice regarding the need for America to get tough on China. Leaning on a compliant media establishment to blanket the population in anti-China propaganda, U.S. leadership, otherwise out of ideas, has decided that a campaign of mass indoctrination is the best shot they have at restoring their crumbling legitimacy at home.

Why has Washington adopted this newly bellicose footing? And why now? This is not all that hard to answer. At the highest level, the political class takes its marching orders from a corporate sector that, in the interest of its profit margins, has decided that the time has come for open conflict with China. From the early 1990s to around 2010, U.S. corporations—led by Wall Street—benefited handsomely from access to Chinese markets.[11] This was a mutually beneficial relationship that was enormously profitable for U.S. multinational businesses, which, as a condition for access, freely signed contractual agreements to share their technology with Chinese companies. While this relationship between U.S. business and China was in place, the national security wing of the U.S. state was drowned out by a flood of corporate profits. But in the wake of the Great Recession, these same Chinese companies gradually became the rivals of their foreign guests, cutting into their profit margins by outcompeting them in local and overseas markets. The turning point in U.S. policy came when the most powerful corporations in America began to see China not as a market, but as a competitor undermining their interests. As the sociologist Ho-Fung Hung observes, "Behind the increasing willingness of the United States to counter China's economic and geopolitical expansion from the Obama to the Trump"—and now, we can add, the Biden—"administration is the same structural condition confronting American corporations." Far from some grand struggle for freedom or democracy, the conflict with China is about maintaining the profitability of U.S. capital.

Still, the imperative to defend the interests of big business presents a certain cognitive dissonance for America's best and brightest. According to elite opinion in the United States, liberal democracy and free markets are naturally superior to centrally planned economies. Communism was always doomed to fail, supposedly, because it cannot work—it is too inefficient, too corrupt, too irrational, it goes against human nature, and so on. Now, embarrassingly, U.S. leaders claim that America, the quintessential capitalist superpower, is in danger of being vanquished by a self-identified "communist" country. This is bad optics, as the consultants would say. Wasn't communism supposed to be a total failure? Were the elite just wildly wrong about the viability of planned economies after all? A soothing moral fable reconciles the contradiction: as an authoritarian country, China could only have reached its current stature by cheating in the international system, unfairly manipulating its currency and stealing American technology. Or, in the Trumpist imagination, by helping the rootless, cosmopolitan elite betray America by abandoning it for China—never mind that U.S. corporate involvement with China merely followed the laws of the capitalist marketplace, seeking out the most profitable returns on their investments. For both camps, innocent America was victimized by the scheming Chinese, a convenient fiction that identifies a national enemy to blame for American decline while ignoring its source: the exhaustion of the economic system that has connected the world under the imprimatur of American power for the last seventy years.

Entropy

For about the first three decades after the end of the Second World War, the rich economies of North America, Western Europe, and Japan experienced a long boom of synchronized, rapid expansion, as the capitalist world rebuilt itself with generous U.S. aid and overseas investment. Protected by the U.S. security umbrella, world trade thrived during the Cold War, bolstered by an international economy based on the dollar, which was itself backed by gold. In the heart of the U.S.-led bloc, which also comprised West Germany and Japan, corporate profits and real wages rose together, carried by high labor productivity rates in their core manufacturing sectors. Examining growth rates can be tricky, because economic data are inherently unreliable, and different countries use different metrics for measuring them. But by the standard measure of gross domestic product (GDP), which measures the exchange value of all products and services bought and sold within a country over a given time, the United States saw the longest sustained boom in its history during this period, with real GDP growth fluctuating around 5 percent annually from 1948 to 1973, although steadily declining year over year.[12] Its strength was closely linked to the dynamism of the larger global order it underpinned.

With the world inflationary crisis of the 1970s, the world growth dynamic began to change. As inflation intensified early in the decade, the dollar came under intense international pressure as demands to exchange dollars for gold eventually exceeded the actual bullion held by the U.S. Treasury. This amounted to a global bank run on the dollar, as governments and private creditors rushed to trade their increasingly worthless dollars for the security of gold. In response, the Nixon administration announced a temporary suspension of the gold standard in 1971, and after a futile attempt to fix it, formally declared it dead in 1973. Fixed exchange rates between currencies on the basis of gold were replaced by floating exchange rates determined by the demand for them on the world market. From this point on u.s. economic growth continued to decline, but its dynamic became closely tied to the financial business cycle: periods of wild expansion driven mostly by frenzied speculation on rising asset prices, followed by financial crashes, waves of bankruptcies, and deep recessions. With each recovery, u.s. GDP growth failed to reach the level of the previous cycle, its average rate gradually trending downward. The u.s. economy came to resemble a giant casino for making money by gambling, even while the overall vitality of the economy deteriorated. This contradictory dynamic culminated in the great crash of 2008, when an enormous international bubble based on inflated housing prices collapsed. In the years following it, annual GDP could barely manage to stay around 2 percent. This broad slowdown is now recognized by researchers and commentators of all stripes, though radical analysts on the left had been pointing to the problem for decades before the mainstream began to acknowledge it.

Mainstream growth figures tell part of the story, but real GDP per capita is a more accurate measure, as it adjusts not only for inflation but for population growth, giving a better sense of how economic growth translates—or fails to translate—into better standards of living. According to the u.s. Bureau of Economic Analysis, real growth per capita averaged 2.3 percent from 1953 to 1973, and 2.0 percent from 1973 to 2007.[13] From 2007 to 2019, per capita growth averaged a mere 0.9 percent.[14] To provide a sense of scale for these numbers, a tenth of a percentage point in national growth could translate into tens of thousands of dollars of annual income for the average person, or tens of thousands of jobs in the larger economy. We will investigate the meaning behind these figures and the various explanations for them in more detail in later chapters, but for now it is enough to note that official data clearly show the waning prospects for broad income and employment growth in the United States.

The decline of the United States parallels the broader stagnation of the global capitalist economy that it leads. From 1961 to 1973, the OECD countries expanded at an average rate of about 4.2 percent per capita, while the rest of the world followed closely behind, according to data compiled by the World Bank.[15] But after 1973 growth begins to fall off, business cycle by business cycle, with the peak of each succeeding period failing to reach that of its predecessor, much less that of the postwar era. It is worth noting, too, that these statistics do not take the costs of capital depreciation—the wear and tear of producer goods and fixed structures like buildings—into account, so the real rate of growth is even lower. Economists and politicians almost universally expected the storm clouds of the Great Recession eventually to subside, allowing the world to revert to its pre-crisis growth trend. Nothing of the sort occurred, and instead OECD growth rates, again tracked closely by the rest of the world, would permanently remain at their new lower level, fluctuating around 1.5 percent and scraping 1.2 percent by the end of 2019, just before the world economy plummeted off the cliff of the coronavirus outbreak. While 2020 was defined by the crisis of the pandemic, in fact the world economy was already heading into recession by the end of 2019. In the official statistics, at least, the decay of the capitalist system is unmistakable.

Perhaps the most remarkable aspect of this secular slowdown is the ironic fact that the macroeconomic conditions for capitalist growth have in many respects never been more favorable. A thirty-year assault on organized labor and the trade union movement has sapped their strength, all but eliminating their ability to check corporate power; real wages for the majority of the working class have stagnated for decades; revolutions in computational and microprocessing technologies supposedly unlocked previously unknown possibilities for innovation and productivity; the world-historical incorporation of India, China, and the post-Soviet sphere brought massive, cheap workforces into the world market; neoliberal politicians happily dismantled national welfare states, privatized public services, and introduced the efficiencies of market competition into ever more areas of life that were previously shielded from it; and the decades-long reign of free-market ideology and its corollary dogma of government austerity cleared the way for entrepreneurial initiative. Paradoxically, the long downturn has taken place in a context approaching what economists believe to be the ideal conditions for a free market economy. Capitalists could not have asked for a better business environment. Far from slowing, growth should have been stupendous throughout the entire era.

While aggregate figures like GDP are a workable if crude measure of economic health, they tell almost nothing about how the income and wealth of a society are distributed. Another generally acknowledged fact is the staggering growth of inequality in the advanced economies, especially pronounced in the USA. In North America, Western Europe, and Japan, the lower middle classes experienced virtually no real wage growth between 1988 and 2008.[16] As is well known, this is in stark contrast to the rich, especially the very rich, who have done exceptionally well. Taking total income growth for the world over the same period, the global top 5 percent took a full 44 percent of it; the top 1 percent took nearly one-fifth.[17] This contrast, already striking enough, becomes even starker when one considers wealth rather than income inequality. Income is the flow of payments one receives from wages, salary, interest, and so on over a period of time; wealth measures the cumulative value of all property and assets, that is, the total market value of an individual. By this measure, the top 1 percent of the global plutocracy owns 46 percent of the world's wealth.[18] This top-heavy distribution is mirrored in the United States, with the top 1 percent of households owning 42 percent, and the top 0.1 percent owning as much as the bottom 90 percent, almost a quarter of total wealth.[19] The lower half of that 90 percent, the American working class, has either zero or negative net wealth. The middle class, for its part, has also seen no net improvement, owning the same share of national wealth that it did seventy years ago.[20] At the same time, declining real incomes have buried u.s. households in a rising mountain of debt, some $16 trillion as of 2022—three-quarters of annual GDP.

By themselves these figures already tell much of the story behind the political chaos and popular uprisings that have shaken the United States and the other liberal democracies over the last decade. These seizures are only some of the most visible effects of the exhaustion of capitalist growth. As growth slows, it increasingly becomes a zero-sum affair, with the gains of the few only coming at the expense of the many, and in a capitalist economy this means sacrificing the livelihood of the vast majority to the need for continuing profitability. This is an important point, because reformers often focus on the uneven distribution of wealth as the main source of society's ills: if we redistribute the wealth then inequality would be reduced, the economy would pick up, and living standards would improve. But as will become clear in later chapters, in reality it works the other way around: inequality is not the cause of economic underperformance, but a *consequence* of it, of the synchronized slowdown of growth worldwide. As a result, standards of living are falling and only set to get worse, the working class is immiserated, and a downwardly mobile middle class is disappearing, all so that a global plutocracy and the corporate order that it represents can continue to enrich themselves. Seen in this context, the period of finance-driven capitalist expansion from the early 1990s to 2008—the era of high globalization—can be more accurately understood as a partially, temporarily successful attempt by nation states to adapt to the declining energy of the global capitalist economy, a trend well underway long before China's rise to global prominence. u.s. decline is not due to the machinations of China or of any other country, but is the result of the fading vital signs of a world system made in its own image, and to which its fate is chained.

The Fascoid Rebellion

The exhaustion of the capitalist system in its current form has shattered the promises of the post-1989, globalized world order. With each passing year the promised growth breakthrough— always just around the corner—does not happen. With this history in view, the worldwide resurgence of tribalistic nationalism appears not so much a revolt against globalization as a convulsion of terminally ill societies. As growth dissipates, mass frustration spreads, and ever more people hold politicians—as those who are supposed to be able to do something about it—in utter contempt. This context is indispensable for understanding the worldwide rightwing backlash, but appears nowhere in the mainstream debate. Instead, liberal commentators mainly see the rightward drift of contemporary politics as the advancing threat of "populism," an ill-defined term serving as a catch-all for any tendency opposing the centrist establishment.

For the nervous defenders of the status quo, so-called populists are irresponsible upstarts who take advantage of the partisan climate to whip up hatred for their own benefit. As it appears to the Princeton historian Sean Wilentz, "Trump and his incipient regime are utterly abnormal. Trump represents a sharp break in our national political history . . . his election the result of a fundamental collapse in our politics."[21] He explicitly rejects looking into the sources of this "collapse," urging instead an investigation into the "elites who whipped up those resentful politics and thought they could exploit them."[22] One can find similar takes in the pages of the *Financial Times* or *The Economist.* For liberals, the problem is bigoted demagogues who fan resentment to disrupt an otherwise healthy republic. But it is the unreconstructed neoconservative right that brings out the full logic of the liberal position. To quote the neocon intellectual Robert Kagan, Trump represents "how fascism comes to America."[23] For Kagan, fascism does not endanger democracy, but is rather *too much* democracy, a tyranny of the crazed majority whipped into a frenzy by a "strongman" who promises to enact revenge on their enemies. Whether it focuses on populism or fascism, the gist of the liberal position is that these tendencies represent no coherent movement or ideology, but are a phenomenon of the rogue individual leader, a schemer trying to achieve dictatorial powers by riding the waves of popular discontent.

Meanwhile, from the other side of the mainstream, conservatives fret about whether populist politicians actually represent a real movement. Michael Lind, an academic and co-founder of the New America Foundation, is a case in point. His 2018 book, *The New Class War,* is anxious to distance Trumpism from the fascist label, and from the tabloid drama surrounding Trump himself, by providing a more intellectually respectable case for it. For so-called national conservatives like Lind, the new class war in America is supposedly between the college-educated "managerial overclass" of the major cities and the more traditionally minded working majority residing outside the metropolitan cores. This new class war supposedly pits the working class, made up of those without a college degree, against an educated, multicultural, higher-income minority, an opposition that conveniently redefines class war as a culture clash between competing lifestyles: the mostly white, church-going masses of the country against the godless, multicultural professionals of the city. In Lind's telling, economic, cultural, and political power come with entry into the managerial class, and with that access comes a shared set of liberal values, like racial diversity, representation, and gender freedom—markers of the hated "identity politics" in the reactionary brain.[24]

Sociologically, the whole argument hinges on the Trump vote representing a cri de coeur of the working class finally standing up to the managerial elite. But far from Lind's Norman Rockwell tale about the virtuous, hard-working heartland victimized by amoral, rich city dwellers, research based on electoral data has shown that a large portion of Trump's constituency is made up of affluent individuals who are not rich by national standards, but *are* rich by local standards, that is, relative to their local community. Basically, the higher one's income compared to one's own community, the more likely one is to vote or support Donald Trump.[25] At the same time, while the 2020 election did see a large increase in turnout for the incumbent across virtually all demographic categories, the anti-Trump turnout, especially among poor and low-income voters, also set records, and was in fact instrumental to the Democratic victories in key states like Georgia, Arizona, and Pennsylvania.[26] Large majorities of working-class Americans apparently despise Trump and the movement he stands for; conversely, locally wealthy, mostly white exurban and rural elites are the backbone of Trumpism. To put a finer point on it: rightwing populism is mostly a movement of the intermediate social stratum known as the petty bourgeoisie, an amalgam of property holders, franchisees, small business owners, and rentiers. It is a movement of the rural and suburban gentry who dominate the working poor across Middle America.[27] Frightened of socialism from below and corporate power from above, it is this wing of the militant, upper middle class that has historically provided the shock troops for fascist mass movements. Not working class but not quite ruling class, and petrified by anxieties of downward economic mobility, the petty bourgeoisie gravitates toward domineering figures who could relieve their fear of insignificance. This is the source of the yearning for submission to petty tyrants that fuels mass authoritarian politics.

This same addled subclass is at the heart of the rightward shift in world politics over the last decade. Europe, where a new axis of hard-nationalist parties has formed governments across the continent, is illustrative. Governing coalitions in Italy and Sweden, two countries with formerly strong social-democratic political traditions, include or depend on parties with literal fascist or neo-fascist roots, the Brothers of Italy and the Sweden Democrats. Both parties have risen to prominence by spouting an acrid mix of hardline immigration policies, welfare chauvinism, and free-market platitudes aimed at an audience of shopkeepers, the self-employed, religious conservatives, and, more recently, frustrated crypto-bros suffering from delusions of grandeur. Italy's current prime minister, Giorgia Meloni, envisions a new Europe re-committed to the values of the "free market" and its traditional Judeo-Christian identity. Italy's Northern League, the Brothers' key coalition partner, built its social base among Milanese mid-size manufacturers outclassed by the multinational megacorporations of Western Europe.[28] For these factions, "free market ideals" in practice simply mean reducing the monopoly power of foreign competitors.

Between these northern and southern poles of the European Union, voters in Central Europe have also returned majorities for hard-right, sovereigntist governments in post-Soviet Poland and Hungary. In power from 2015 until late 2023, Poland's Law and Justice (pis) party caters to a base of small- to midsize business owners, sole proprietors, and wannabe entrepreneurs who feel constantly under attack from big Polish and European firms. Law and Justice bewails the plight of the "poor little Polish entrepreneur," while claiming to defend Polish families beset from all sides by evil elements like foreign corporations, LGBTQ+ activists, and immigrants, especially refugees.[29] To the east, Viktor Orbán's Fidesz party rails in official Hungarian media against the European Union, against Jewish billionaires like George Soros, and their supposed immigrant and LGBTQ+ allies subverting the nation from within, none of which stops his government from welcoming big Western European banks and manufacturers as the largest employers in the small post-Soviet nation.

Like Trumpism in America, all of these regimes appeal to a popular base with petty-bourgeois, middle class, and religious voters as their foundation, with portions of a disoriented working class signing on in favor of figures that at least say they will do something different from the decades of austerity that came before. In the event, very little actually changes. Despite his reputation as an anti-EU firebrand, Orbán is happy to receive billions of euros in the EU's lavish agricultural subsidies, which he promptly disperses to well-connected cronies close to the regime.[30] He seems disinclined to change his economic policy, which basically amounts to selling the Hungarian population as a cheap workforce for German car manufacturers, indeed treating the Hungarian economy as little more than a colony for West European capital. The Polish government promised a post-pandemic recovery plan that would fuel economic growth with a generous public spending program in favor of ordinary citizens, funded by EU relief funds and taxes on high earners. Instead, unsurprisingly, the tax hit lower-wage workers hardest, while benefiting the highest earners.[31] The popularity of Law and Justice is fading in the wake of the cascading crises following the COVID-19 pandemic, which led to the defeat of their parliamentary coalition in the elections of October 2023. And in Italy, Giorgia Meloni's EU-bashing regime has promised not to jeopardize the massive $200 billion post-pandemic recovery fund granted to Italy by the EU. Despite its market-loving, anti-bureaucratic ideology, the Brothers of Italy are more than ready to accept funding from the same villainous, international cabal supposedly oppressing the Italian people. All of these countries are dependent on EU financial support because they remain trapped in a larger, downward cycle of declining productivity, investment, incomes, and growth. Imposed by a deteriorating international economy, these structural constraints sow the misery that pushes people to elect so-called populists out of desperation, leaders who have no real program or remedy to alleviate their condition—indeed, there are none. But the Orbáns and Melonis of the world are at least willing to titillate their followers by reprising the revanchist, proudly racist rhetoric of the original fascist movements.

Anti-Politics, Then and Now

Poverty, frustration, fear, and promises to wrest national sovereignty back from the global elite—we have seen something like this before. As the curtain fell on the first cycle of capitalist globalization from 1815 to 1914, the original fascist movement of interwar Europe emerged under the pressure of crushing economic breakdown, which disorganized the traditional ruling classes and opened up the political space for fascist parties to contest them. The term itself was coined by Benito Mussolini in 1919, shortly after the conclusion of the First World War and the outbreak of the Russian Revolution, as Italy was shaken to its foundation by a sweeping social crisis. "Fascism" came to describe a paramilitary movement that would unite the nation by violently pacifying the conflicts within it—especially labor conflicts. In this sense, it was a form of political extremism aimed at the depoliticization of society.[32] Fascists agitated for an alliance between workers and capitalists, their rhetoric an ambiguous blend of anti-elitism, heroic nationalist mythology, a belief in natural hierarchies, and productivism, the notion that national strength comes from classes cooperating to boost industrial activity. But its most distinctive ideological feature was hysterical hatred of the left, especially the international socialist left. In Italy, this posture earned Mussolini's movement the early backing of the big rural landowners, as well as a base of popular support from shopkeepers, middle-class professionals, clerical workers, and the broader, patriotic middle classes—that is, the petty bourgeoisie. This was the formation that carried Mussolini to power in the March on Rome in October 1922.

Likewise, in the short-lived Weimar Republic, Hitler's National Socialist German Worker's Party (NSDAP, otherwise known as the

Nazi Party) gained momentum by promising to resolve the divisions within German society, destroy the left, and restore national
greatness.[33] But the Nazis encountered a major obstacle to their
plan. In the decade after the First World War, Germany's powerful
industrialists were more invested than their Italian counterparts
in free multilateral trade. While happily in favor of domestic
repression to stabilize the business environment, many of them
distrusted political extremism, especially the Nazi emphasis on
an unpredictable, militaristic foreign policy prosecuted through
a big, centralized state. For Germany's liberal-minded capitalists,
such things were likely to disrupt international markets and
dampen their profit outlook. But this attitude began to change
around 1930 when the international economic situation started
to rapidly deteriorate. As the Depression intensified, the collapse
in world trade effectively cut the ground from beneath the feet of
German economic liberalism, leaving corporate bosses with no
compelling reason to oppose the handover of power to the Nazis.
Moreover, the hierarchical Nazi worldview based on top-down,
unquestionable authority nicely chimed with their preferred view
of the natural relationship between capital and labor. In effect,
the worldwide depression had broken up the material basis for
liberalism, allowing fascist political goals to align with the class
interests of capital.[34]

Classical European fascism succeeded by fusing the fear and
frustrations of the middle-income strata with the profit-seeking
agenda of big business. This class alliance is the heart of fascism.
But certain objective conditions are needed to transform it into
a political movement capable of seizing state power. In Italy,
an international, postwar situation defined by deep social crisis
and a wave of revolutionary uprisings threw the country into
chaos, making the fascists seem appealing to industrialists, big
landowners, small business owners, and the military. In Germany,
the Great Depression was the *global* environment that gave
German ultra-nationalists the opportunity to enlist big business

in a coalition with the petty bourgeoisie. As when compression raises the temperature of gas molecules by pushing them into more frequent collisions with one another, the contraction of a deep economic depression agitates class conflicts, ratchets up social fear, and allows hyper-nationalist militarism to appear as the solution. The slow-motion collapse of the world market was the condition of possibility for the original fascist takeover.

If the thirty-year cycle of war and depression lasting from 1914 to 1945 was the murderous conclusion of the British-led "long nineteenth century," then the current, worldwide revival of suffocating economic stagnation and spasmodic nationalism is the slow death of the post-1945 U.S.-led international order. But key elements of the original fascist formula are missing. With the important but partial exception of the Russian invasion of Ukraine, calls for national salvation through full-scale war have not yet materialized. Rightwing paramilitary violence has resurfaced, but has not yet taken institutional form in political organizations. Most importantly, though, the global economy remains mostly intact. Measured in terms of international trade volume, globalization is slowing, but it has not stopped, much less reversed.[35] If an enduring collapse in the world economic system is a necessary condition for ruling classes to resort to the fascist political economy, to the economics of full, national self-sufficiency, then such a turn has not yet materialized. What *has* materialized, under the pressure of the geopolitics of competition and white, middle-class discontent, is a pronounced rightward shift of the center of gravity of politics. This is not because fascist movements have acceded to state power, but because dominant factions of the corporate elite, especially in the capitalist system's most powerful representative, the United States, have leveraged the atmosphere of popular anger to push for a type of state-sponsored capitalism more aligned with their interests.

In the United States, a relentless crisis cycle has eroded the traditional social advantages of the white middle-income classes and small business owners. While Trump became the vessel of disinherited white rage, his idiosyncratic nationalism, particularly its anti-China themes, dovetailed perfectly with the outlook of a business sector itself increasingly dissatisfied with the international status quo. As U.S. firms lost ground to their Chinese competitors, influential members of the ruling class decided they were done with the idea of free trade, and were ready for the U.S. state to prosecute a more aggressively nationalist foreign policy on their behalf. Thus the Trumpist revolt presented a historic opportunity for corporate interests to realign state policies into a more aggressively nationalistic posture. While Trump himself was too unpredictable for the stewards of U.S. stability at home and supremacy abroad, his bumbling brand of national chauvinism became the state's chief strategy for pacifying the domestic revolt he himself symbolized. Trumpism rapidly became the elite consensus of both major political parties because it allowed state actors, particularly in the national security sector, to fulfill two objectives at once: to undercut the threat of charismatic, populist leaders and to single out China as the scapegoat most responsible for U.S. decline, all by doing what U.S. corporations already wanted them to do. Given this convergence of social forces, the executive wing of the U.S. state determined that confronting and subjugating China is the best strategy to secure domestic stability, as it co-opts the revanchist narrative at the heart of Trumpism while offering the best shot at slowing the trends behind a rapidly deteriorating domestic situation. By adopting a reckless, egomaniacal foreign policy, state actors hope to neutralize the turmoil destabilizing the country, to depoliticize U.S. society, by satisfying the needs of their real masters, the corporate elite. As in the 1930s, it is decaying global economic conditions, not ambitious populist leaders, that vanquish the pretense of liberalism.

Slowing growth, intensifying competition, anxious bureaucrats, and the disappearing relevance of the white middle classes: these are the intersecting tendencies that are pushing Western politics rightward. Discarded as the guiding framework for international relations, liberalism is all but dead, euthanized by its own defenders. The new dispensation is every country for itself. Domestically, Western governments increasingly claim to rule for a narrowing tribe of the true people: true Poles, true Italians, real Americans. Despite the rhetorical radicalization, policymakers remain mostly helpless in the face of a secular, transnational trend of economic decline, and unable to improve the lot of the majority of the people. In the absence of any socialist alternative, this trajectory of desperation is only headed in one direction. While genuine fascism has not yet taken power, this is the broad and open way by which it might. Such is the unpromising context in which flailing politicians have revived the call for "industrial policy," the topic of the next chapter and a notion—like fascism—long seen as a relic of less enlightened times.

three

Eclipse

In the spring of 2021, the newly inaugurated Biden administration announced a sweeping agenda to combat climate change, calling it an "existential threat." On its first day of office the administration had already signaled that the United States would rejoin the Paris Agreement—the global climate accord struck in 2015, from which the Trump administration had withdrawn the United States in its own first year. In April 2021, the u.s. government seemed ready to recommit to the cause, rekindling its traditional self-image as the leader of the international community after the embarrassments of the Trump years. The administration announced its intention to pursue what amounted to a green industrial policy, pouring government resources into pioneering post-carbon industries and kickstarting a broad, equitable economic recovery. The implicit scope of the program and the scale of government spending it would take were remarkable. "America must lead the critical industries that produce and deploy the clean technologies that we can harness today," the administration stated in a press release, "and the ones that we will improve and invent tomorrow."[1]

Yet only a few months later the mood was very different. The Biden Administration gave the green light to drilling for oil on federal land even faster than had the industry cretins appointed to the Department of the Interior by Trump. While the administration did nix the infamous Keystone xL pipeline, this was the exception proving the rule, as it subsequently backed a slew of sprawling new pipeline projects. Its signature "bipartisan" infrastructure legislation allocated $25 billion of fresh subsidies to the fossil fuel industry, which already enjoys extravagant public funding, while also pouring money into new and expanded highways for gas-guzzling trucks and automobiles. Despite its determination to pursue hydraulic fracking as a key domestic source of energy, the U.S. government still found itself practically begging OPEC and Russia to flood the world market with oil in a desperate bid to cap rising fuel prices.[2] All this was well before the outbreak of the war in Ukraine, which exacerbated the price spike and renewed the government's supplications, particularly to Saudi Arabia, traditionally a key U.S. ally. But these pleas had little effect. Ignoring them, OPEC decided not to raise but to cut oil production, intensifying upward pressure on energy prices.[3] By October 2022, the United States had grown desperate enough to come hat in hand to Venezuela, whose government it had tried to overthrow just a few years earlier, offering to lift sanctions on the beleaguered country to get the oil flowing again.[4]

The same contradictory pattern plays out across the world. Flouting the U.S.–Mexico–Canada trade agreement struck in 2019, the Mexican government has opted to shun U.S. and Canadian clean energy companies in favor of its state-run oil firm, Pemex, and its own Federal Electricity Commission.[5] Mexican president Andrés Manuel López Obrador promotes a doctrine of national energy sovereignty that doubles down on petroleum and coal and has little room for private, foreign investment in renewables. In the European Union overall carbon emissions have been trending downward, but Germany, the EU's leading power, remains an enormous consumer of natural gas, as well as a major burner and exporter of coal. Burning natural gas does not emit as much carbon as coal or oil, but it does release huge amounts of methane, a powerful greenhouse gas in some ways worse than CO_2 itself. But industrial exports are central to Germany's political economy, and German industry needs cheap fuel sources to remain competitive. India, the world's third largest carbon emitter behind the United States and China, has so far refused to endorse a net-zero carbon emissions target, flatly declaring the development of the economy to be the higher priority. This can hardly be a surprise: India's private capitalist sector has nearly become moribund, staying alive mainly through continuous lavish funding from various government subsidies.[6] Even the cartoonishly reactionary regime of Jair Bolsonaro committed Brazil to a 50 percent emissions reduction by 2030, though the regime continued to deforest the Amazon in the pursuit of lucrative mining and agribusiness exports. The Chinese government has pledged that the country will be carbon neutral by 2060, and China is the world's largest producer and exporter of wind and solar energy. Yet, as part of the government's efforts to power a national economic recovery following the pandemic, the country is currently burning more coal than the rest of the world combined.

Virtually everywhere, the widening consensus on the need to address the ongoing catastrophe of climate change is shoved aside by the imperative to remain economically competitive. It is the same with the need, demonstrated by the coronavirus contagion, to collectively confront emergent pathogens that literally pose a biological threat to every human being on the planet. Crises on a scale that jeopardize human civilization itself are clearly understood as such, even by the elite, but at the same time it seems taken for granted that not much can be done about them. Instead, in a world in which growth is scarce and ideas scarcer, industrial policy has made a comeback, not as a pathway to some egalitarian, post-carbon social democracy but as something that capitalist countries are forced to adopt to defeat one another on the shifting stage of global competition. Its return to fashion in official discourse marks a distinctive feature of that competition in the current moment: a constantly expanding footprint of national states in both national and international corporate economies. As economic growth slows down, states are compelled to abandon the usual platitudes about free trade, openly calling for the kinds of aggressively nationalist, beggar-thy-neighbor policies that the world was supposed to have left behind.[7]

All of this augurs not just the end of post-Cold War globalization, but the definitive end of an entire era of u.s.-led world capitalism. If the universal expansion of markets, free trade, and open capital flows was a project underwritten by the u.s. state since the end of the Second World War, as the historians Leo Panitch and Sam Gindin document in *The Making of Global Capitalism*, then the reversal of this trend and the return of industrial policy worldwide marks the abandonment of that project.[8] What the authors of that excellent history did not foresee is that the United States itself would become the undertaker for the political order it supervised for almost three-quarters of a century. Far from trying to prevent the unmaking of global capitalism, the United States now leads the charge to demolish it.

Bugs in a Jar

Until quite recently, the very notion of industrial policy was anathema to u.s. policymakers. The concept has a long history in the modern era as a way for national governments to pursue rapid growth by prioritizing certain key sectors, and has played a major role in both developing and advanced economies. After the Second World War, for example, France and Japan practiced "indicative planning," in which the government set out long-term goals for specific sectors as well as overall growth rates, and used policy to help guide the private economy toward them. Through industrial policies, governments channel funding and resources into targeted sectors in order to shift the overall structure of the economy toward those sectors. It entails making strategic decisions about which industries are most important and then actively supporting them to achieve better growth outcomes than would be possible under strictly market-led competition. In short, industrial policy is a form of state intervention in the economy; not the market, but the government picks the winners. Even the United States practiced such policies in the postwar era, deciding to prioritize cars over mass transit, to develop nuclear power, and to construct the monstrous fusion of business and government known as the military-industrial complex.

Supposedly the world had long grown out of the need for active governmental planning, having left it behind a half-century ago in favor of market-led growth. Now it is back in fashion. This is a bitter pill to swallow in a country like the United States, where official dogma firmly holds to the assumed superiority of free markets over planned economies. Some intrepid reactionaries face the cognitive dissonance head-on. *American Investment in the 21st Century*, a report commissioned by Florida Republican senator Marco Rubio, is worried about "the long-term direction of the American economy." Rubio, a born-again Trumpist, insists that the profit-driven market economy was "our biggest competitive advantage over the failed, centrally controlled socialist economies of the past, and should continue to be over China and other competitors of the future."[9] Yet he also notes that since the late 1970s U.S. corporations have mostly bought financial assets instead of investing in the kinds of productive operations that generate good jobs, a debilitating trend that has left the country in its current sorry state. Uncoincidentally, the period of financialization Rubio identifies exactly parallels the rise of market fundamentalism in the United States. As is well known, from the early 1980s to the late 2000s, the elite consensus in Washington was that there is no alternative to the free market, to use Margaret Thatcher's famous motto. The innovative spirit of business would lead the way to greater shared prosperity if government would just get out of the way. Indeed, it was just this ideology applied to banks and other financial institutions during this period that, by creating massive new opportunities for profit, opened the floodgates for the great shift toward financialization that Rubio is criticizing. The unqualified rule of the market, "our biggest competitive advantage," led directly to the present, miserable state of the u.s. economy.

Rubio does not dwell on the irony. In the preface to the report, he is quick to invoke the threat of "our adversaries, who are wasting no time in securing their own economic futures," especially China, which is doing everything it can "to win the technologies of the future—robotics, artificial intelligence, advanced pharmaceuticals, and 5G." The implication is that the United States should be doing the same. To foster national capital development, America must ape the tactics of its allegedly inferior enemies, rejecting the outcomes of the market and actively managing them toward national ends. Rubio calls for a values-based system that would encase markets in governmental and cultural institutions, as "economic guidance can only be as efficacious as the value system which shapes it."[10] In other words, social cohesion is no longer to be sought through free commercial exchange, the realm of civil society that has traditionally defined liberal culture since the eighteenth century. Rather, it is to be sought in some cultural substance, some fundamental set of values or essence that supposedly defines the national tribe, especially against its official enemies.

The communitarian turn on the American right reflects the same objective conditions that are bringing the idea of industrial policy back into the political mainstream around the world. According to the United Nations Conference on Trade and Development's *World Investment Report 2018*, the number of states adopting some form of industrial policy or targeted interventions within strategic industrial sectors is also increasing rapidly, and "appears to be at an all-time high."[11] China is perhaps the most well-known case, but the European Parliament, concerned to counter the aggressive green energy subsidies of the u.s. "Inflation Recovery Act" passed in 2022, has also launched its own "EU Industrial Policy."[12] Germany has released its "Made in Germany 2030" industrial policy, mimicking China's "Made in China 2025" program.[13] Emmanuel Macron, president of France, announced that the French state will soon need to "take ownership in several industrial sectors" to strengthen the country's independence.[14] Indian prime minister Narendra Modi assumed office on a slate of promises to unleash market-led innovation and creativity to revive India's economy. Since then, the regime's growth strategy rapidly reversed into a pantomime of industrial policy, devolving into a frantic free-for-all of subsidies to businesses and trade tariffs in a bid to raise India's manufacturing share of GDP—which, despite all that, still remains at a twenty-year low as of 2019.[15]

All these cases are a throwback to the policy approach of the 1950s, when planning was at its height in the capitalist world as both a policy regime and an ideal. Planning was then widely accepted as part of "scientific management," the standard equipment of modern states by which a well-trained bureaucracy could tame the extremes of the capitalist business cycle. The most optimistic among mid-century intellectuals even saw the perfection of planning as the key to solving the basic economic problem of scarcity. For the optimists, the bounty of state-guided growth would unlock material abundance and ever more inclusive welfare services for all, eventually removing most, if not all, of the need for competition in the economy altogether. Planning represented not only an economic technique but the promise of plenty, maybe even the road to a post-capitalist future.[16] Since the 1970s, however, neoliberal governments across the world believed they had left such notions behind as the childish dreams of a misguided era.

No longer. Evidently the executive managers of the capitalist state now have no other option than to return to the state-driven development policies that modern societies were supposed to have left in the dustbin of history. Only, unlike in the twentieth century, these policies are not accompanied by a vision of progress, some plan to manage or even overcome the miseries of life in capitalist society. Instead, vacuous government officials haphazardly dip into the toolkit of the past in a desperate bid to revive the fortunes of private capitalism, merely to keep it alive, with little idea what they are doing or where we are headed. Industrial policy has returned in the wake of the abject failure of the world capitalist system to generate sufficient growth to maintain the status quo. With growth mostly exhausted, state actors are forced to adopt these policies on an ever-larger scale, which become the vehicle through which the major powers vie for control over the remaining sources of growth. When you shake a jar with insects in it, they will fight as they are thrown against one another. The global capitalist system is like such a jar, and we— the people of the countries within it—are violently thrown up against each other with each world-shaking crisis of the system, which grow more severe with each passing year. The only solution is to get out of the jar, or perhaps to break it.

New Imperialisms

In contrast to the happy days following the close of the Cold War, when Thomas Friedman was penning his paeans to globalization and the spread of liberal democracy and free markets would supposedly lead to an era of prosperity for all nations, the main theme of elite thinking in America today is the renewed need for protectionism in a zero-sum world. It was not all that long ago that commentators enjoined us to think of the China–u.s. relationship as "one economy called Chimerica," as the economic historian Niall Ferguson and the economist Moritz Schularick put it, "the sum of China, the world's most rapidly growing emerging market, and America, the world's most financially developed advanced economy," the symbiotic link at the heart of a globalized world.[17] Their timing was auspicious. Writing in 2007, the authors were concerned to address the credit crunch that had begun in the summer of that year, an ominous sign causing some trepidation in world financial markets. The authors reassured their elite audience as only members of the economics profession can, concluding that, after all, "in our view, [the credit crunch] does not portend an implosion of an equity market bubble comparable with the dot-com era."

Now, in the wake of over a decade of cascading crises, and especially following America's embarrassingly inept management of the coronavirus pandemic, these same commentators chatter incessantly of the need to confront or even decouple from China as a matter of national security.[18] Ferguson himself has forgotten his old portmanteau of yesteryear to trumpet the "New Cold War" with China. As one would expect, the theme of national self-determination is accompanied by a revival of national chauvinism. Ferguson points to the advantages such a new cold war could bring, as allegedly, during the previous Cold War, "domestic divisions decreased considerably" in the face of a common external foe. In the spirit of bipartisan cooperation, both the Republican and Democratic parties have embraced the story of a global struggle of democracy (whose avatar, naturally, is America) against the evil forces of authoritarianism, represented most vividly in the American imagination by China and Russia, cast as rogue violators of the "rules-based international order."

In China itself, the escalating confrontation with the United States is narrated from a standpoint identifying with the interests of the Global South. Invoking the legacy of the revolution, official Chinese Communist Party (CCP) discourse casts China as a champion of development and equality for the poor countries, the historical victims of colonial conquest and exploitation. In this discourse, China only aims peacefully to continue its economic development as a responsible member of the international community, and it is the United States, with its turncoat pivot from free trade to belligerent mercantilism, which is the real rule-breaking rogue of the global order.[19] Official propaganda in contemporary Russia is in some ways similar. The Russian government casts its military aggression not only as a pre-emptive, defensive measure against *Western* aggression, but as an act of defiance against a self-serving, unipolar international order led by the United States, which, of course, has its own illustrious history of launching pre-emptive invasions of other countries. In the eyes of these countries' leaders, it is rank moral hypocrisy when America condemns unprovoked military attacks or defends the sanctity of human rights, since America itself launches such attacks and undermines such rights whenever it is expedient to do so. (To acknowledge these facts is not to justify the actions of these countries; it is simply to acknowledge reality.)

Foreign distrust of the United States is well warranted. After all, neoliberal globalization happened under the aegis of American power. In fact, it was a continuation of the same project for global governance that the nation had been pursuing since the mid-twentieth century, which aimed at opening up an ever larger space for capital and commodities to flow freely across the planet with the United States at its center. Leo Panitch and Sam Gindin refer to this project as the "political economy of American empire."[20] Starting in the 1940s, American policymakers identified the interests of the u.s. state with the health of this global capitalist order, the architecture for which it had conceived and constructed as part of the Bretton Woods agreements in July 1944. In the aftermath of the Second World War, that order consisted mainly of the United States, Western Europe, and Japan, but following the end of the Cold War, the opportunity arose to fully globalize this project.

After 1989, governments that wished for their countries to participate in the world market—to join the so-called "free world"—were expected to undertake the raft of policy measures the economist John Williamson dubbed the "Washington

Consensus." These are the familiar, laissez-faire policies of flexible exchange rates, reduced government deficits, liberalized capital markets, openness to foreign direct investment, and privatized public assets—the commercial pillars of global capitalism. By happy coincidence, most of these freedom-enhancing reforms opened up lucrative profit opportunities for u.s.-based companies, while also bringing a wider swathe of the world into the dollar-based international order centered on the United States. But crucially, as Panitch and Gindin point out, incorporation into this order was attractive for participating countries because it seemed to offer real opportunities for economic development.[21] This made it different from previous imperial formations: the United States was the hegemon of an "informal" empire, based not on direct territorial control but on participation in a world market designed largely by u.s. prescription.

For some theorists, though, there is nothing informal about it. The economist Michael Hudson describes these arrangements in his widely read book, *Superimperialism*. In Hudson's story, u.s. security and monetary officials stumbled upon a new way of exercising monetary dominance after dropping the gold convertibility of the dollar and ending fixed exchange rates in 1973. Despite America's growing indebtedness and declining industrial competitiveness, severing the link with gold strengthened the dollar as the global reserve currency by making u.s. state debt into the world's new monetary base. Hudson defines American "superimperialism" by the deepening indebtedness of the principal imperial power. The u.s. borrows by selling Treasury securities, which allows the government to drive up its current account deficit through madcap spending on imports and a bloated, world-spanning military without worrying about budget constraints. The rest of the world is coerced into absorbing this deluge of Treasury debt by explicit threats of military force and financial sanctions, as well as the implicit threat that refusing to fund the u.s. budget deficit would put the world monetary system itself at risk of breakdown. Foreign purchasers of u.s. debt thus fund their own exploitation. "It is not to the corporate sector that one must look to find the roots of modern international economic relations as much as to u.s. Government pressure," Hudson writes. "At the root of this new form of imperialism is the exploitation of governments by a single government, that of the United States, via the central banks and multilateral control institutions of intergovernmental capital rather than via the activities of private corporations seeking profits."[22] Superimperialism is driven not by economics but by politics, the overriding imperative for the United States to expand its imperium. Power exists for the sake of getting more power. Plainly tautological, Hudson substitutes a provocative description for an actual explanation.

Hudson captures an obvious aspect of u.s. financial power. The usa enjoys higher global demand for its sovereign debt and for securities denominated in its currency than any other country in the world by far. But as an account of imperialism the story suffers from some elementary deficiencies. There is a single agent, the United States, which unilaterally imposes its monolithic will upon the rest of the world. Other countries are not actors, but passive objects. This precludes any understanding of how other countries might tangibly benefit from these arrangements, or leverage them into forms of competition or even counter-hegemony. Likewise, any divisions or conflicting interests within America itself, in its government and society, and how these might affect its policies, are dissolved into a unipolar description of the United States oppressing everyone else. Ultimately, these weaknesses stem from Hudson's basic concepts, which abstract entirely from the realm of production, of social and material life, to articulate a purely financial theory of imperialism. In this conception, finance and industry are not interwoven in an intricate political economy. Rather, finance is the antithesis of industry, existing only as a parasite on the host of the "real economy." In the context of the new Cold War, this sets the stage for a supposed struggle between American-sponsored neoliberal financialization and China's "industrial socialism," as Hudson labels it.[23] Amounting to the slogan "capitalist finance bad, capitalist production good," anti-imperialism is reduced to endorsing the national ideology of a rival great power.

Not all accounts of contemporary imperialism focus on the United States. If Hudson provides a theoretical justification for the current policies and self-understanding of the People's Republic of China (PRC) regime, then the economists Michael Pettis and Matthew Klein have provided a rationale for an aggressive U.S. trade policy in their macroeconomic study, *Trade Wars Are Class Wars*. Klein and Pettis contend that the global economy is suffering from entrenched structural imbalances in which the excess savings of a few low-consumption, highly productive economies—mainly China and Germany—fund excess spending in high-consumption, trade deficit countries, such as the United States. The productive countries' obsession with export-focused trade policies leads to suppressing consumer demand in China and Germany, where workers do not have the incomes to consume the majority of what they produce, or to support large volumes of imports from the rest of the world. This generates enormous current account surpluses. Collected by the government and deposited in its central bank, these surplus savings are then channeled through financial markets to buy assets and fund credit-fueled consumption in the deficit countries, which allows the surplus countries to continue dumping their excess products, with the USA "acting as a sink for foreign gluts."[24] The result exacerbates inequality in both sets of countries, as artificially suppressed demand in the export economies keeps wages low while inflating financial incomes and asset prices for the rich in the importing economies.

Unlike the financial account of "superimperialism," this Keynesian analysis at least has the virtue of incorporating macroeconomic dynamics rather than assuming them away. Drawing inspiration from the British economist J. A. Hobson's classic theory of imperialism, which argued that low domestic demand encourages manufacturing interests to channel capital into colonial markets abroad, Klein and Pettis effectively reverse the superimperialism thesis. Far from being the dominant imperial power, the United States has become the victim of export imperialism, fueled by the irrational desire of European and East Asian elites to hoard their wealth. Accordingly, the onus is on these countries to restructure their economic model for the good of the global economy. But why do elites hoard? According to the authors, elites simply "prefer to accumulate financial assets."[25] The rentier seems to have an urge to save for the sake of saving that needs no analysis. This urge cannot explain much, or acts at best as an unexplained first cause. Although it is not their intention, the authors provide a convenient rationalization for the core Trumpist narrative of American victimization, and its corresponding wish to revive economic growth in America by forcing other countries to adjust to its preferences.[26]

As in most Keynesian theory, the global crisis boils down to a lack of effective demand. Low rates of capital investment are due to persistently weak demand across virtually all major economies, a dearth of consumer spending power caused by the desire of venal elites to hoard their savings. Enlightened government administrators should redistribute the economic surplus to ordinary consumers in Germany and China, and undertake a program of fiscal stimulus, especially by building infrastructure, in the United States, to restore global equilibrium. The "irrational political constraints" that have held down demand and investment would be removed, resulting in a rebalanced world economy in which investment could once again become rational, defined by the authors to mean "seeking out the most productive opportunities around the world," instead of mere speculative gains.[27] Yet this conclusion makes little sense given the authors' own logic. If wealthy elites enrich themselves at popular expense because they prefer to do so, it is not clear why they would change their behavior simply because some smart economists suggest they should. For that matter, why would governments, who gave them sanction to do so in the first place? The practical conclusion contradicts the argument's premises.

Though these two accounts of imperialism appear to be polar opposites, they have much in common. They share the premise that politics determines economics, grounding their explanations of economic phenomena in political decisions rather than political economy, in an analysis of how the global product is distributed instead of how it gets produced in the first place. This, in turn, is possible because both take the state to be something separate from the economy, an institution intervening in or responding to the economic system from outside of it. They also share a common notion of imperialism, which is construed as one (or several) nations exploiting others by taking more than their fair share of global wealth. And they are both nationalist theories, which is a logical consequence of their basic concepts. In the context of escalating geopolitical conflict among the world's most powerful countries, they pose a choice between rival great powers. But this is a false choice.

All of these shared features are rooted in a common blind spot. Globalized, combined, and uneven production, the transnational foundation of the capitalist system, is either considered from a purely technical standpoint, as in the Keynesian frame, or it is all but invisible, as in the theory of financial imperialism. This treatment leads both perspectives to misunderstand the role of u.s. pre-eminence in world capitalism, which is either greatly overstated or completely ignored. Consequently, even as the United States itself tears down the very system it championed for the better part of a century, neither is equipped to understand the deep dynamics driving the premier capitalist superpower to end global capitalism as we know it. It is not the case that political actors can control the key economic relationships that set the limits of the policy options at their disposal. Neither, though, are they mere functions of these constraints with no room to act creatively. Rather, they make history, but under conditions inherited from the past they have not consciously chosen. These conditions are the forces and relations of world capitalist production. Their evolution does not mechanically determine politics, but, in tandem with it, reshapes the relations between state and economy in ways that alter the nature of both.

Profit and Pillage

The geopolitical terrain of the world economy is defined by the interplay between international cooperation and national competition within a single system of production, the capitalist system. In this system, the productive resources of society are privately owned and are put to use to employ people and produce things only if they yield a profit for their owners. The arrangement usually looks like this: an employer hires people through a wage contract. The laborers work with the tools, raw materials, equipment, and facilities owned by the employer to make a product, which belongs to the owner, who then sells it for more than he initially paid for the labor and the means of production. The worker gets her pay, the owner gets the profit, which is what he retains after deducting his costs from the final sales price. It seems straightforward, but there is more going on beneath the familiar fact of wage work for profit.

What exactly is profit? Despite having studied the question for over two centuries, there is still no general agreement among academic economists.[28] In ordinary perception, profit is simply the return from a successful business transaction, total revenues minus total costs. This is, in fact, how businesses calculate their net income, which neoclassical economists call accounting profit.

But economists also have their own definition of profit, which includes not only the actual costs of business but opportunity costs, or the potential revenues a business gives up by choosing to use its resources in one particular way rather than another. To take a salient current example: a publicly traded company might want to spend money on capital expenditures to produce actual things, but by doing so it misses out on the chance to buy back its own stock from its shareholders, which by reducing the ratio of outstanding shares to earnings immediately improves the company's profitability. Economists count this missed opportunity as a cost of the company's decision to pursue productive operations, and so factor it into its net earnings. The point of this definition of profit is to capture the idea that in a perfectly competitive market, with perfect knowledge of all options by the market participants, all such missed opportunities will be eliminated over time, as businesses make the most efficient use of their assets until there are no further gains to be made. From this point of view, profits are incidental, an outcome of impure competition resulting from short-term informational or technological advantages. In the long-run equilibrium of perfect competition, all such advantages eventually disappear, reducing profits to the cost of doing business. Yet neither the accountant's nor the economist's definition of profit explains the most distinctive feature of modern economies, which is their tendency to ceaselessly expand, for capital and profits to constantly grow.

A simple example can illustrate the problem. If a company profits by buying something cheaply and then selling it for a higher price, then that is a gain for the seller, but an equal loss for its buyer—the profits from the higher sale price are taken at the expense of its trade partner. So the net outcome of the exchange for the whole economy is zero. In other words, the gains from exchange do not account for any net growth of the economy. Where does growth come from, then? Pointing to his models, the economist will insist that total profit growth is not the rule, but the exception, since in a market economy all profits should, in principle, be competed away. An expanding economic surplus has to be accounted for by factors supposedly external to the economic system, like technological innovation, population growth, or the excess market power of corporate and government monopolies. For most academic economics, the most empirically observable and striking fact of the modern economy, its endless growth, is taken as a special case that can only be explained through a series of exceptions.

Instead of proceeding in this backward way, Marx's approach to profit analyzes the dynamics of growth as a matter of the capitalist process of production, for which the accumulation of profit is not the exception but rather the basic purpose of its existence. Because they are guided by this purpose, corporations have a natural incentive to obtain the largest possible profit by making their workers work harder for less money. But Marx's point is that even aside from such explicit forms of exploitation, workers produce profit as a built-in feature of their relationship to capital. Workers are paid the minimum necessary to sustain their labor power, their ability to work every day for the corporations who exploit them, as well as to reproduce themselves over time. This minimum—Marx calls it the value of labor power—is socially and historically variable, reflecting the technological development, educational level, cultural norms, and other factors that influence the cost of living in a given society at a given moment. At the same time, employees paid the value of their labor power work for longer than would be necessary to reproduce that value. That is, on a given working day with a certain social level of productivity, the worker reproduces the value of the wage she is paid, together with something additional to that value, for which she is not paid. This additional value, which Marx calls surplus value, is the origin of what we know as profit.

Capitalist businesses can enrich themselves through the accumulation of profits because of this production of surplus value. Close up, the wage relation appears as a contract an individual owner and an individual worker enter into for their mutual benefit. At the level of the whole economy, however, it is a relation between two classes, in which one of them, the workers, by reproducing themselves, also generate the growing economic surplus that is the system's most distinctive feature. Waged employment is the arrangement through which the entire class of workers produces the social surplus that is then distributed among the owners as a class, who give some of it back as wages while keeping the remainder for themselves as profit, interest, rent, dividends, and so on. These revenues can then be reinvested to hire more labor and expand the means of production, to accumulate more capital. As reproducing this class relationship is essential to the system, the interests of the capitalist owner class are identified by default with those of the larger society, of the nation and its government. This is where the role of political power comes into play.

Entanglement

Marx assumes the value of labor power roughly equals the wage because he assumes a capitalist economy that reproduces itself over time, which requires reproducing the workforce. But capitalists themselves, caught up in the practical work of profit-making, have no interest in reproducing or even understanding the requirements of the broader system. Because the pursuit of profitability under competitive conditions demands economizing on costs wherever and however possible, individual corporations have a natural interest in paying their employees the lowest possible wage, or, what amounts to the same thing, forcing them to work as long and as hard as they can for a given wage. The interest of the boss is to minimize what economists call unit labor costs, or how much they must pay their employees to produce one unit of output per period. Ideally this ratio would be as close to zero as possible, which would entail wages well below the value of labor power. Before the advent of the standard eight-hour workday, this was the norm, with workers in industrializing countries commonly working twelve-hour, thirteen-hour, or even longer shifts of backbreaking, mind-numbing factory work for a mere pittance—barely enough to survive. Such low wages undermine the foundations of the capitalist system by endangering the source of profit. Yet whenever corporations can get away with it, they are happy to pay less than a living wage, and leave it up to the workers to figure out how to survive.

A society organized on a capitalist basis can only materially reproduce itself if the specific social relations of capitalism are preserved and reproduced, yet normal corporate behavior tends to undermine those very relations, destabilizing the continued accumulation of profits. At the same time, extreme exploitation stokes class hatred from the workers it depends on, who, facing such conditions, may decide that the whole arrangement of production for profit is more trouble than it's worth, and organize to overthrow it. This is why governments of the industrializing countries began to intervene in their national labor markets in the late nineteenth century, inaugurating a trend that reached its apogee in the welfare states built in the years following the Second World War. State agencies, and the bureaucrats who run them, are neither the neutral regulatory apparatus imagined by Keynesian theory nor a monolithic structure of oppression, as imagined in Hudson's superimperialism story, but rather sprawling, half-organized efforts to contain the problems thrown up by the contradictory tendencies of private capitalism. The capitalist state is the political form of the social relations of capitalist production. Government welfare laws are a case in point.

Take the landmark social-welfare laws passed in Germany in the 1880s, which in many ways provided the blueprint for the national welfare states that arose in the twentieth century.

From the squalid wage slavery of the urban factories emerged an assertive, politically conscious workers' movement that did not just demand a living wage, but the abolition of wage labor itself. As the German Social Democratic Party (SDP) put it at their founding Gotha Congress in 1875, their goal was "to effect the destruction of the iron law of wages by doing away with the system of wage labor." Facing the rapid growth of the SPD, five years later the government of the new German Empire, led by Chancellor Otto von Bismarck, began to pass a suite of laws fixing the length of the working day, inaugurating health and workplace accident insurance, and outlawing child labor as well as work on Sundays. Bismarck was no friend of the workers, but as the first chancellor of the Empire he was concerned to establish social peace between labor and capital that would strengthen the industrial competitiveness, military strength, and international stature of the German nation through the development of German capitalism. In this context, welfare legislation formed part of the state's effort to safeguard the overall conditions of profit-making not just from a radicalizing working class, but from the self-destructive behavior of the profit-makers themselves. Through their legal interventions in the social relations of production, governments entangled themselves with the private economy, becoming part of the process of reproducing it.

These interventions need not take the specific form of welfare legislation. For officials at the highest executive levels of the government, the point of regulating domestic conflict is to secure the conditions for the profitable growth of the country's corporations, which is to say to preserve the basis for the rule of the bourgeois class. This class, whose combined assets make up the national capital of the country, is mainly interested in making more money, for which it enlists the services of the state to help prosecute commercial wars against the ruling classes of other nations. National governments enthusiastically comply, since their existence is inextricably tied to the health and vigor of their domestic capitalist class. Governments remain subservient to this class even as they strive to organize and strengthen it against its international competitors. There is competition within the capitalist class, but in its political interventions, the national state strives to define a unified, coherent interest for the class as a whole.

The leaders of Japan's Meiji Restoration of 1868 understood this very clearly, after overthrowing the Tokugawa Shogunate in the name of modernizing the economy and the military so that Japan could meet the threat of Western imperialism. Unlike Germany, Japan had no democratic mass movement of industrial workers exerting pressure on the government. What the new regime did have was an unusually open opportunity to design Japan's capitalist institutions almost from scratch. The Meiji government closely studied the economic history and industrial methods of the Western nations. It then embarked on a series of modernizing measures, eliminating feudal domains of land tenure and converting them into government property subject to tax, creating modern private property rights for peasant landholders, establishing universal education, and, most sweepingly, abolishing the traditional caste order to replace it with a national market in free wage labor, so that anyone could take any job. The government constructed the foundations for the social relations of capitalism at a record pace, compressing a historical process that had taken centuries in the West into a couple of decades.

For the Meiji regime, time was of the essence, as it was also confronted with a surplus population of peasants and warriors (samurai) left over from the old feudal order. For an embattled regime striving to secure its rule following a violent coup d'état, roaming groups of disgruntled warriors and peasants were a major concern. In a kind of proto-welfare program, some of the now-purposeless samurai were paid a government stipend. But for the rest of the feudal remnants—the remainder of the samurai, peasants, tenant farmers—employment had to be found, or made.[29] The new government met two goals at once by establishing state businesses to employ the newly created labor force in key industrial sectors such as transportation (railroads), communication (telegraphs), mining, textiles (particularly cotton), shipbuilding, military weaponry, chemicals, glass, and construction. It even intervened in time itself, modernizing traditional Japanese clocks, which had hours of variable length, to the standardized Western day consisting of 24 hours of sixty minutes each.

While operating initially at a loss, the new state industries laid the basis for heavy industrialization, a long-term undertaking that the nascent private sector could never have pursued on its own. The companies closely connected to military and national security remained under state control, but the rest were sold off at firesale prices to private financial houses, forming the basis for the *zaibatsu*, the industrial-financial conglomerates that are the bedrock of corporate Japan to this day. Then, after taking over the state-founded industries, Meiji-era employers had the advantage of a laboring population that could subsist on relatively low wages.[30] Combined with the government's push for general education, a low value of labor power made it possible to greatly economize on capital investments by using proportionally more labor for industrial operations than in more capital-intensive Western nations. This state-driven approach to development enabled exports from these operations to pay for the import of foreign machinery and advanced technology that would lay the basis for Japan to accelerate into the large-scale, industrial manufacturing that became the core of its economy by the early twentieth century.

The cases of Germany and Japan illustrate how politics has become entangled with what Marx calls the forces and relations of capitalist production. The state does not adjust the parameters of the economic mechanism from the outside. It is itself a massive gear in the capitalist machinery, constantly working to dissolve the obstacles to the further growth of corporate profits. At the same time, the state attempts to manage the class struggle by presenting itself as the guardian of the general interest of society, apart from the economy. One of the capitalist state's essential features is its role as a supposedly disinterested party arbitrating between different, formally equal interests. It must maintain the appearance of neutrality as a condition of its political legitimacy. This tension between securing the conditions for the ongoing corporate plunder of the population, on the one hand, and securing the conditions for the continued loyalty of that population, on the other, is a problem that the capitalist state can never resolve but must constantly strive to manage one way or the other.

As these cases also suggest, heavy industry has a unique role in the history of capitalism. Industrialization introduces a new growth strategy that is one of capitalism's most distinctive features: the tendency to constantly revolutionize the technical aspects of production. Instead of extending the period of surplus labor time directly by forcing workers to accept lower wages and longer hours, large-scale industry expands the surplus indirectly by replacing humans with machines, mechanizing the production process. Once the working day and the value of labor power are stabilized, mechanization becomes the general mode of surplus value appropriation—it becomes the internal motor of the production process. Through mechanization, the same number of workers can produce a greater output per unit time; alternatively expressed, less labor produces the same output. This key ratio of time worked to produce one unit of output, normally measured as a sum of money, is the rate of labor productivity. Other things being equal, higher rates of labor productivity correlate with higher rates of profit, a result of the enlarged scale and volume of production. (Note, however, that the source of profit in *surplus* labor time is obscured, as the ratio only sees the relation between total time worked and the product it yields.)

The pursuit of ever higher productivity has led to the introduction of heavy industry in countries around the world, as governments and companies attempt to copy the perceived success of industrialization in raising national incomes. As mechanized techniques become generalized, as the economy becomes organized around industrialized mass production, the overall productivity of labor increases. One of its most important effects, in turn, is to increase productivity in the sectors making the products and services workers need to sustain themselves, lowering the value of these products and, with them, the value of labor power. To lower this value is to reduce the portion of the workday in which the worker reproduces the value of her labor power, and so to extend the time during which the worker works for the boss for free. This dynamic, generalized through the international spread of industrialization, becomes the engine of the mindless drive for productivity that defines the course of development in, and the conflicts between, capitalist societies.

Overproduction and World Politics

Particular corporations in particular countries mechanize their operations to raise their profit rate by increasing labor productivity. As these techniques become generalized, the relative advantage for their early adopters dries up, and a new productivity norm becomes the rate at which businesses must produce to remain competitive. The drive for a new breakthrough in productivity begins. Enormous amounts of profit are produced and realized during this process while workers are deleted from it—that is, by getting rid of the real source of profit, labor power. As a result, even as individual corporations rake in more money through investing in machinery, the average rate of profit for all producers declines. The longer this goes on, the scarcer profitability becomes, further intensifying the pressures of competition. The result is a permanent tendency to overproduce capital relative to the size of the market.

Economists—like businesspeople—see market competition as the driver of corporate technological innovation, but the competitive pressures of markets, especially the world market, are as much the *consequence* as they are a cause of the drive for greater productivity, which as a rule outpaces what markets can absorb. As the scale of production expands and labor power shrinks as a share of total expenditures by private business, total profits worldwide will also tend to shrink relative to the total invested capital. The resulting fall in industrial profitability is a well-documented empirical trend. In the book *Capital Wars*, for example, the financial analyst Michael J. Howell records an overall decline in the returns on industrial capital from 1984 to 2019 for Germany, the United States, and China, with the rate of return in all three countries nearly converging by 2019.[31] Likewise, according to the World Bank, growth rates for industrial "value added" in the three countries have slowly converged on a common downward path since the early 1990s.[32] Value added is the net output of a sector, or total output (sales) minus intermediate inputs (purchased components, energy, raw materials, services), so it can serve as a rough, indirect indicator of profitability. In the long run, the declining average rate of profit is the other side of the growing scale of capital investment, of the capitalist pursuit of ever greater productivity. Corporations experience this trend as heightening competitive pressure to remain profitable. This conflict between productivity and profitability plays out internationally in the competitive arena of the world market, where corporations and their national governments experience it as a problem of foreign competitors. By colluding to improve competitiveness by investing in additional industrial capacity, states and corporations only exacerbate the original problem of overproduction.

Examining the history of the postwar international capitalist order is instructive. What would eventually become the globalized production economy of the neoliberal era that emerged in the 1980s was built atop the ruins of industrial warfare inside the advanced capitalist core. Having exited the Second World War with all of its industrial capacity intact and all of its chief rivals laid waste, U.S. industry enjoyed pre-eminent status in the middle of the twentieth century. Its workers manufactured products in factories that represented the world technological standard for efficient mass production. Leveraging its industrial strength as well as its position as the world's largest creditor with the biggest gold reserves, the U.S. government set out to construct an international order centering on the U.S. dollar and based on the open flow of products and capital. Ideologues publicly talked about this as an imperial project. As the editors of *Fortune*, *Life*, and *Time* magazines proclaimed in a statement issued in 1942, the coming U.S.-led world order would be a "new American 'imperialism' . . . quite different from the British type." To the authors, this would be a new type of empire, one based not on direct rule over foreign territories but on the spread of "free enterprise" under the imprimatur of American power.[33]

Yet precisely because of its central role within this order, U.S. industry was steadily undermined by rival German and Japanese corporations that gradually came online with postwar reconstruction. As the trade barriers in place since the end of the Second World War were gradually dismantled, these late-comers to the world market for manufactured exports like steel, automobiles, and electronics benefited from lower wages as well as more efficient machinery that represented the next generation of production techniques. Crucially, they enjoyed open export access to the enormous U.S. market, where demand consistently ran hot thanks to Keynesian stimulus policies, including spending for the murderous campaign in Vietnam, up through the late 1970s. Such open access to the U.S. home market as well as overseas markets at the expense of U.S. exporters was encouraged by the U.S. government as part of its Cold War foreign policy, which required strong anti-Communist bulwarks in Europe and East Asia.

This geopolitical strategy could be sustained as long as markets were expanding and profits growing for all producers. But once the bulk of postwar reconstruction was complete, this condition ceased to hold, since as market expansion slowed, manufacturing export growth in one nation increasingly had to come at the expense of others. The result was an intensifying case within the u.s.-led industrial bloc of what is sometimes called "export imperialism," but which is really just part of the normal course of capitalist competition. Mutually beneficial trade relationships between the industrialized nations turned into a hyper-competitive battle over markets propelled by the growing overproduction of capital, a situation in which existing export markets became insufficient to support the existing productive capacities. Zero-sum economic logic kicked in, making competition no longer complementary, but conflictual.

As a consequence of their technological edge and lower wage levels, the newer European and Japanese industrial corporations earned higher rates of profit at the expense of their obsolete u.s. counterparts, which were duly decimated. These higher profits—just like those of u.s. corporations in the preceding period—represent value not directly produced by such firms, but rather value captured. That is, the massive profits that businesses earn competitively producing for the world market represent value appropriated not from their own workers directly, but from the global pool of money produced by exploited labor worldwide. International economic competition between nations is a conflict over this global surplus.

To see how this works, consider the hypothetical case of a single country as a closed economy, before bringing in the international market. Such an economy will have a wide range of different kinds of business using different combinations of capital resources and labor. Since the surplus value produced by the use of labor power is the source of profit, the branches employing relatively more labor at a high rate of exploitation produce the bulk of the surplus value; conversely, those with proportionally more machinery than workers (those with higher labor productivity) will produce less. But this does not directly correlate to their respective profit rates. As one would expect, corporations that invest more in materials, equipment, facilities, and advanced technology will typically earn a higher rate of profit, since they will have lower labor costs, greater efficiency, and so on. Their high profits are an appropriation of the surplus value produced by the system as a whole, which they get as part of the money received from sales.

The money corporations earn from sales does not sit in a safe in their corporate headquarters, but flows into their accounts held at the major national banks, forming a pool of surplus value for the economy as a whole. Banks use this pool as a basis to provide credit to all of the businesses collectively, to the capitalist class, for further investment and expansion, as well as to workers to buy the stuff capitalists produce. In this way, the credit system helps form an average rate of profit across the economy, as investment tends to flow into sectors with higher than average profits, eventually pushing them down through excess supply; this then makes the rate of profit in the other sectors appear comparatively appealing, which attracts funds to them, other conditions being equal. Total surplus value is distributed across the economy as competition compels investors to seek at least the average rate of return on their investments. Most importantly, insofar as capitalists continue to ratchet up labor productivity through mechanization, the source of surplus value gradually dries up. Over time this brings about the problem of overcapacity by eroding the source of profits in the exploitation of labor power, placing downward pressure on the average rate of profit for all the country's corporations. Lower profits mean capital expenditures make less sense for the owners of money, pushing down rates of investment. Stagnation and crisis lie not far ahead unless a remedy can be found, perhaps abroad, outside the country's borders.

Now let's zoom back out to look at the actual world market again. The general pattern laid out above works the same way in this context, only it takes place among companies within different countries, introducing international politics directly into the processes of competition and accumulation. States will aid their corporations to improvise and experiment however they can to counter the falling profits of private capital, which in the world market are determined not nationally but internationally.

For example: during the Cold War the capitalist world was engaged in an internal war of export imperialism. Until 1971, U.S. dollars served as world money, pegged to gold at $35 an ounce. As U.S. private profits eroded under the pressures of manufacturing overproduction, its economy stagnated, fueling inflation, which began to accelerate in the 1970s. When the governments of the other industrial powers—Germany, Japan, and France—sought to exchange their less valuable dollars for gold, this put tremendous downward pressure on the dollar, further exacerbating inflation. Underlying these events was a steady downward fall in the private profit rate in the industrial economies, which had fallen by 20 percent in the G7 countries together and a full 30 percent in the United States from 1965 to 1973.[34] As both the leading steward of the international capitalist system and a particular nation state, the United States had to balance the relationship between its global responsibilities and its political legitimacy in the eyes of its national population, two roles that were frequently in tension with each other.

In the wake of the inflationary tide that engulfed the capitalist world following the abandonment of the gold peg and fixed exchange rates in the 1970s, the Keynesian elite, trained in the "scientific" methods of demand management, found themselves unable to stabilize national economies with the traditional remedies of state spending and tax cuts. The resulting impasse opened the door to radical monetary approaches that an earlier generation of economists had dismissed as crank nonsense. In 1979 Fed chairman Paul Volcker set off the "Volcker shock" to the economy, limiting the money supply and allowing interest rates to float freely, limited only by what the market could bear. The resulting depression, triggered by skyrocketing interest rates, eventually broke the trend of rising prices in consumer products, while inaugurating an era of constant inflation in the prices of financial assets. However, high interest rates put tremendous upward pressure on the dollar, crippling u.s. manufacturers while bestowing a major competitive advantage on foreign rivals. Consequently, the United States prosecuted industrial warfare against its trade partners via the Plaza Accord of the mid-1980s, when it unilaterally imposed unfavorable and devastating trade terms on Japan and West Germany to secure greater market share for its own manufactured exports.[35] The agreement engineered higher exchange rates for the German mark and Japanese yen, enabling the dollar to fall from its historic heights. By way of the shakeout of excess industrial capacity—and, of course, massive layoffs—that followed the deep depression of that period, this strategy did restore profitability to a newly consolidated u.s. industrial sector by imposing devastating recessions on its foreign rivals.

National competition, in sum, is competition over the global surplus product. Monetary policies, tax laws, corporate subsidies, and trade agreements are some of the measures states take to assist their national corporations in raising profitability, that is, in capturing more of this global surplus. "Imperialism" is not defined by the direct domination or exploitation of one country by another, but is the name for the international hierarchy through which the competitive struggle of capitalism plays out. As the form of this struggle, imperialism is just business as usual in the capitalist world economy. But as explained earlier, the system's built-in drive to raise productivity slows the growth of the surplus, making global competition into a zero-sum conflict by default. The capitalist world system is like a circular firing squad in which the pursuit of productivity by all participants results in general desolation for them all.

The Planetary Factory

At the same time, the competitive process is an engine of both ruin and renewal. Competition and crisis drive the ongoing evolution of capitalism as an economic system, as well as the political order that regulates it. Throughout the postwar era, U.S., European, and East Asian producers funneled profits into their banks, where they formed massive pools of money capital. Following the takeoff of financial liberalization policies in the late 1970s, which removed barriers to the flow of money capital across currencies and continents, this common fund enabled capitalists to seek out higher returns on industrial investment by relocating to areas that allowed for combining newly mechanized production techniques with lower labor costs. Much U.S.-based manufacturing relocated to Western Europe, South America, Southeast Asia, and the American South, where wages were much lower than the more unionized North; German companies began to rely on cheaper labor in Eastern Europe and the former East Germany following the fall of the Iron Curtain; and Japanese manufacturers made a concerted push for foreign direct investment into South Korea and China beginning in the 1970s, playing an especially timely role in China's economic opening-up period. The thickening concentration of capital in production and its financial centralization laid the groundwork for today's multinational corporations to dominate the world market through legal forms like contract manufacturing, management techniques such as just-in-time production, and, of course, cheap labor. These factors defined the terms in which developing economies sought to integrate themselves into the world market through global value chains (GVCS).

The international concentration of production through GVCS that slowly came together starting in the 1970s and eventually found its center in Southeast Asia was driven forward by capitalists struggling to resolve the problem of profitability. But it could only resolve the problem in the short run, exacerbating it over time. Again, this is due to the nature of capitalist growth. The rate of profit sets a limit on what kinds of, and how much, investment is possible. Each successive wave of mechanization in the means of production, each step up in automation as capitalists pursue ever higher levels of labor productivity, expels workers from the technologically dynamic sectors of the economy, eroding the source of profits in the consumption of labor power and resulting in a growing population of economically redundant humans. With each successive wave of industrialization, deindustrialization, and regional relocation, production grows more concentrated, requiring larger volumes of capital, since the growing proportion of investment going into machinery and materials raises the necessary scale of investment. Barriers to entry rise while the basis for further capital accumulation narrows, and the global pool of money capital with dwindling outlets for investment gets bigger.

The reorganization of the world's productive system into GVCS is one of the most distinctive features of the world wrought by globalization. Manufacturing via GVCS relies on sprawling transnational networks for extraction, processing, manufacture, assembly, and transportation in which primary materials, intermediate components, and final outputs are each moved through dozens of countries in a meticulous division of labor to produce a single commodity. Mostly connecting the countries of North America, Europe, and East Asia, these fragmented networks are involved in 80 percent of all imports and exports between these regions, including both intermediate and final products, but are concentrated among just 15 percent of their private corporations, according to figures from the World Bank.[36] For any given product, especially those with complex technological components like phones and computers, dozens of countries can be connected through one labor process. At the same time, these countries and their affiliated corporations remain economic competitors with one another, seeking constantly to gain or maintain advantages over their rivals to capture a larger share of the profit opportunities the system presents.

Throughout the 1990s and early 2000s GVCs expanded at a dizzying clip, an arrangement benefiting from the widespread deregulation of global trade and investment during those decades. Their growth, and the participation of developing countries within them, was an important part of the Whig narrative of globalization that neoliberals liked to tell themselves, as it would allow the realm of free trade to steadily expand beyond its original postwar nucleus of the United States, Western Europe, and Japan. Participating in these value chains would allow developing countries to specialize in a few key areas in which they have an advantage, supposedly, which would lead to better outcomes for all trade partners. For example, this could be inexpensive raw materials, a low-cost and/or educated workforce, or a particularly favorable geographical location. Involvement in GVCs would allow developing countries to become familiar with foreign technology, increase their exports, raise their national incomes, and evolve into modern, industrial economies. At the same time, the advanced economies benefited from the lower production costs and cheap imports GVCs made possible. Governments of developing countries only needed to liberalize their economies by removing barriers to international trade and investment—including, of course, offering "flexible" (that is, non-unionized) workforces—and global financial markets would do the rest by allocating capital to its most efficient uses.

It all seemed a decisive confirmation of the classical theory of trade, articulated by David Ricardo, which stated that specializing in areas of comparative advantage always results in higher net gains from commercial exchange between countries, so it is always in their interest to trade on the basis of specialization. Globalization seemed to open a new path to what development economists used to call modernization, the idea that all nations could progress along the course of development to eventually join the club of high-income countries. The optimistic narrative was fueled by some remarkable developments, notably the rise of China. During the decades in which the PRC government relaxed its direct control over the economy, built up large internal markets, and opened up to international investment, China's economy grew at a dramatic, historically unprecedented pace.

However, while markets played an important role, they were only one instrument within a much greater state-driven project of development. The key condition for China's world historical economic ascent, its attractiveness as a global manufacturing hub, was the foundation laid by the state socialist policies of the Mao years, which had created a literate, skilled working class unparalleled in its size and quality. The PRC government leaned into this advantage with domestic policies that tightly regulated labor markets, such as the *hukou* system, which prevents the country's tens of millions of migrant workers from collecting social benefits in the industrial municipalities where they work. The tradition of central planning inherited from the collectivist period, based on the Soviet model of "big push" industrialization structured by five-year plans, enabled Chinese policymakers to see the market not as an end in itself, but as one tool in a long-term project of modernization.

Taken together, these features of the Chinese political economy made it possible for the country's southeastern coastal regions to become the workshop of the world in what economic geographers call the "new international division of labor." In the old or "classic" division that characterized international trade during the nineteenth and twentieth centuries, developing countries of the periphery mostly provided primary commodities and raw materials to the industrialized metropolitan countries, which were organized around technologically sophisticated manufacturing labor that allowed them to sell higher-value products back to the periphery. In contrast, the new division of global labor is characterized by the concentration of manufacturing in Southeast Asia, with China at the center, including lower-skilled, labor-intensive production as well as higher-skilled, heavily automated factories, while the Global North is increasingly organized around consumption, the mental labor of product design, intellectual property rents, services, and deindustrialization. Importantly, the "old" global division of labor coexists with the new, as the rapid industrialization of Southeast Asia fueled a commodity supercycle of primary products, energy, and raw material exports from suppliers in South America, the Middle East, and Africa. Combined with this structural transformation in the geography of global production, the legacy of state socialism allowed China to become capitalism's flagship success story during the 1990s and 2000s.[37]

But as we know, China's development did not lead to the happy future imagined by the economists, or by the Western political and business leaders who welcomed the country into the World Trade Organization in 2001. Instead, international trade slowed dramatically following the Great Recession and has been stagnating or shrinking ever since. China's recent re-casting as a global villain by the high-income countries was prompted by this slowdown and the numerous social crises it has introduced in them. The share of GVCs in total world trade peaked in 2007–8 at just over half, having plateaued since then and begun to fall. Overall international trade growth between 2007 and 2016 was only half what it was from 1990 to 2007.[38] Foreign direct investment (FDI), through which corporations invest in subsidiary operations outside their country of origin, is a key index for tracking the health of international commerce and connectivity. As measured by the Center for Economic Policy Research, total FDI by multinational corporations has steadily declined since its peak just before the global financial crisis of 2008, unevenly but consistently falling year by year before plummeting off a cliff with the COVID-19 pandemic.[39] Statistical research indicates that the persistent stagnation in rates of international direct investment is driven by the paucity of returns on private capital. According to the same data, the declining trend in international investment is accounted for by falling average rates of return on FDI in developing economies, which has resulted in a lower level of total FDI for the global economy than in the mid-1990s.[40] It no longer pays for capitalists to invest in long-term, physical operations in developing markets. As a result, most foreign investment capital now avoids less-developed areas and flows mainly between the North Atlantic countries. Development is going in reverse.[41]

These trends constitute a structural barrier to the continued reproduction of the international productive system as it currently exists. Moreover, according to the World Bank's *World Investment Report 2020*, $11.3 trillion in FDI had already been directed into developing countries at the end of 2019. Economists sometimes estimate the "depreciation rate" for fixed capital, the rate at which production equipment is worn out and needs to be replaced. Assuming a depreciation rate of 3.9 percent, these countries will need an additional $440 billion just to replace depreciated FDI capital, before fresh investment could even become profitable again.[42] Given the already meager levels of FDI coming from the rich world, this hardly seems likely.

Mainstream growth theory claims that some slowdown as economies advance is normal, because as capital grows more abundant, the return on it decreases. This prompts outward investment toward less-developed countries, where capital is scarcer and so its return higher, ideally leading to the efficient distribution of capital across the global economy. But precisely the opposite has been happening. Despite the fact it is normally seen as a less dynamic economy with lower rates of growth than developing markets, the Eurozone still attracted far more u.s. outward FDI than developing markets over the last decade.[43]

The persistent stagnation in rates of FDI complement a similar investment slowdown within the developed economies. Even mainstream economists have recognized the problem, pointing to a persistent issue of "secular stagnation" in the high-income countries. In the United States, the rate of non-financial corporate investment has plummeted over the last two decades—as one recent study observes, "The u.s. non-financial sector is profitable, but it does not invest."[44] If it remains profitable, where do the profits come from? Much of the profit of u.s. corporations is the product not of capital investment in productive activities but of centralizing corporate ownership across the national economy, of corporations profiting from capturing more market share within existing economic activity, on the one hand, and from using their outsize market power to set high mark-ups on prices, on the other.[45] According to the authors of an extensive study of corporate centralization and capital underinvestment in the United States, this profit strategy began

> around the turn of the twenty-first century, [when] the nature of u.s. product markets began undergoing a fundamental change . . . the market share of the four largest public and private firms has grown significantly for most industries, and both the average and median sizes of public firms, that is, the largest players in the economy, have tripled in real terms.[46]

One of the biggest corporations in the world, Microsoft, basically produces nothing, relying almost exclusively on monopoly positions in certain product markets, rents from intellectual property, and acquisitions of other companies to fuel its revenue growth. In short, profits come not from physical investment but from centralization, from expanding ownership by eliminating competition. The authors conclude that intensifying centralization of ownership is extremely profitable, but barely makes use of existing assets, much less fresh physical investments.

While this is undoubtedly true, it is only half the story, as it leaves out the larger context in which such monopolization has occurred—the planetary factory. Dominant u.s. multinationals like Apple, Caterpillar, and Wal-Mart outsource most if not all of their supply procurement and manufacturing to off-shore contractors. Their market dominance comes not so much from centralizing ownership as from access to the lower-wage workforces of other countries, which enabled them to strip down their operations to the bare essentials—a model known as "lean production."[47] A corporation like Apple, nominally a manufacturing company, can own no factories of its own and instead rely on its subcontractors to handle productive activities; this frees Apple to focus on areas like research and development, product design, and financial investments. Taken together, these developments dramatically reduce overall costs, boosting profits accordingly, but such profits remain rooted in physical investments, that is to say, in the exploitation of labor. Companies that follow this economic model are heavily dependent on the continued profitability of their suppliers, which in turn depends on subdued wage growth among the suppliers' own labor forces. But as long as the pattern holds, u.s. corporations can rake in considerable profits without the need to invest very much in additional productive capacity, and so profitability can remain relatively high while investment continues to stagnate.[48]

Lastly, consider China again, the heart of the planetary factory built upon the foundation of the new international division of labor. As did its predecessors in the advanced economies of North

America, Europe, and East Asia, China is undergoing a long-term cycle of industrial development fueled by an initial surge of immigration from the countryside to urban manufacturing centers, followed by a gradual hollowing out of manufacturing cores as the capitalist pursuit of relative surplus value reduces the amount of labor power in the factories. A phenomenon described by mainstream economists as "premature deindustrialization" is plainly visible in the old industrial zones of the northeast, as well as newer centers on the southeast coast such as Dongguan, which has seen "an emptying out reminiscent of places like Detroit, with population density dropping and industry simultaneously mechanizing and fleeing to cheaper or more skilled locales."[49] As explained earlier, such displacements yield locally higher operating profits for the individual firms, but eventually result in less total profits to be distributed across the broader system, a trend plainly visible in China's economy today: according to an exhaustive empirical study by the geographer Phillip Neel, the rate of profit in China has indeed been steadily declining since the Great Recession.[50] China's economic development over the last three decades is a compressed image of the development and decline of the global capitalist economy over the last three centuries.

Epitaph for an Era

What we knew as "neoliberalism" was essentially the political administration of the planetary factory. Its free market ideology and laissez-faire approach to governance could only last so long as the factory continued to hum along more or less smoothly. Growth was bound to slow once the bulk of the factory's surplus had been pumped out and distributed between the nations competing over it. Now the slowdown is shaking the established order to its foundations, like an earthquake ripping through a dilapidated city. This tremendous, subterranean shift is the underlying cause of the end of America's informal empire and the return of economic nationalism.

For three-quarters of a century the United States government assumed the main responsibility for managing a worldwide system premised upon opening the channels of commerce and integrating the companies and countries of the globe into a single world market. American political elites identified the interests and prestige of the U.S. state with that system, managing it on U.S. terms; now they define U.S. interests against it, giving up even the pretense of free trade. Instead of integrating the world market on its own terms, the United States is now the principal country disintegrating it, enacting protectionist policies whose most important effect will not be to revive the U.S. economy, much less the world's, but to set off a ruinous arms race of competing regimes around the world. In this context, transnational crises that demand transnational solutions, such as anthropogenic climate change, are held hostage to the new agenda of gonzo nationalism. Or they are even weaponized by it, as demonstrated by U.S. subsidies to its own energy industry in corporate welfare legislation like the so-called Inflation Reduction Act (IRA).

Plainly violating World Trade Organization rules against domestic protectionism, the IRA is meant to challenge China's dominance in the green energy sector as much if not more than to actually address the climate crisis. It may even make the crisis worse by raising the manufacturing cost of clean energy technologies like electric cars.[51] At any rate, the IRA was supposed to transform the U.S. economy by upgrading and expanding its manufacturing sector, but instead, output in the sector contracted for twelve straight months after its passage—the longest such contraction since the Great Recession. This is consistent with the secular decline of labor productivity in U.S manufacturing, which has been flatlining or falling since about 2010.[52] Far from growing, manufacturing employment is projected to decline dramatically in the years to come, according to the Bureau of Labor Statistics.[53]

On its own terms, the celebrated rebirth of industrial policy in the United States appears to be failing spectacularly.

In the meantime, the policies have of course triggered a chain reaction toward similar protectionism and subsidies in other countries, including the key American "ally," the EU. Avoiding such isolationism was one of the main rationales for the Bretton Woods agreement in the first place, which sought to prevent the re-emergence of the economic conditions that led to the Great Depression and the Second World War. U.S. officials are well aware of the consequences of this course of action, but—like their peers in other countries—feel they have no choice but to pursue it. Under the pressures of a decaying world economy, the lessons of history are easily forgotten. So too are the received truths about "responsible" government, which include the state's relationship to that weird but familiar fixture of modern life: money.

four

The Money Theory of the State

"No domination is so easily borne, even so gratefully felt, as the
domination of high-minded and highly educated officials."

— GEORG FRIEDRICH KNAPP[1]

Franz Kafka's unfinished final novel, *The Castle*, can be read as
a parable about the misrecognition of power. In the course of
trying to discover if he has, or has not, been appointed as a land
surveyor by the local authorities, the protagonist, K., becomes
obsessed with the authorities themselves, the officials of the
great castle whose shadow looms over the village below. Its
bureaucrats cut nearly superhuman figures, working tirelessly day
and night on countless cases while keeping track of innumerable
files with an otherworldly zeal that overawes K. and the villagers,
who respect and even revere them. Over the course of the
narrative, though, it becomes evident that all this strenuous
paper-pushing might be completely pointless, directed to tasks
they may never complete, involving problems and questions that
cannot be resolved or perhaps never existed in the first place—
including, probably, K.'s appointment. The officials might very
well have no idea what they are doing, or they might be useless
drones, working themselves to death in busy work that never
goes anywhere. But for K. this is unthinkable. For their prestige
flows from the impersonal rule of the mechanism, the calcified,

methodical procedures that, as in a cage, enfold and dominate the officials and the villagers alike. K. deploys his own formidable powers of reasoning to penetrate their mysteries in his quest to gain permission to enter the castle. But the more he learns, the more he calmly reasons and deduces the state of affairs with impeccable logic, the more transfixed he is by the officials' cabbalistic aura, the more entangled he becomes in their intricate networks of influence, and the more he effectively dominates himself.

Kafka's paradoxical presentation of modern power drama-tizes the motif of alienation: something unintentionally created by people that takes on a life of its own and dominates them. In Kafka, the governing authorities are less the source than the confused custodians of this obscure power, which comes from elsewhere—perhaps only from the imagination of K. and the villagers. Yet K. cannot resist attributing quasi-divine qualities to the authorities. He cannot help fetishizing them, investing them with the super-ordinate knowledge to decide his fate. The bureaucrats appear to be masters of technical control, when in fact they, like K., are subordinated to the same system of rational irrationality.

The Castle was written in 1926, around the same time another ambivalent theorist of official authority, John Maynard Keynes, was developing the ideas that would eventually coalesce in a new language of capitalist governance. Like K., Keynes took it as an article of faith that state functionaries could govern in the serene name of reason, floating above the messy conflicts of the market economy in order to manage it for the good of the "national community." Also like K., Keynes looked to rational authority for salvation, specifically to a scientifically trained state bureaucracy equipped with a theory which, if competently practiced, would optimize economic growth and more equally distribute its fruits. If all went well, the villagers would be happy.

Appearing in 1936, Keynes's most influential work, *The General Theory of Employment, Interest, and Money*, was aimed at the most pressing ill afflicting the industrialized economies at the time: grinding, chronically high unemployment. The *General Theory* was widely taken to have overturned the dusty doctrine of laissez-faire, the notion that markets regulate themselves to optimum effect. Keynes considered this to be "a bit of metaphysical thinking," and instead placed the national government in a leading economic role as the fiscal agent whose unique spending power and control over investment "will prove the only means of securing an approximation of full employment."[2] Today, in a similar time of global crisis nearly a century later, Keynesian fiscal remedies are popular again, as governments mine the past for something to replace the shattered hegemony of neoliberalism.

As a case in point, take the controversy around modern monetary theory (MMT), a way of conceptualizing money that has influenced debates about fiscal policy in the United States. As interest rates sat near zero in the years leading up to the COVID-19 pandemic, MMT gained popularity among progressive pundits and politicians for insisting that government spending is not constrained by a budget, in the traditional sense. Cutting against mainstream economic thinking, which sees excessive government deficits and rising debt as an inflationary danger, MMT argues that a government issuing, borrowing, and collecting taxes in its own currency can spend as much money as it wants, so long as it is a "fiat" currency neither tied to a commodity like gold, nor pegged to another foreign currency in a fixed exchange ratio. Governments fundamentally differ from individuals in this way. As a taxpayer, your spending is constrained by the amount of currency in your bank account; for the government that issues that currency, however, no such limit exists, because unlike you it can essentially create money out of thin air, and then get others—like you—to use it.

To invoke the lingo, such a "monetary sovereign" can, and therefore should, create and spend as much as it needs to secure full employment and mobilize all available resources in its economy, regardless of deficits and limited only by the need to keep inflation under control. For example, this could include a jobs guarantee to provide a government job to everyone who is unemployed and willing to work. "Countries with monetary sovereignty, then, don't have to manage their budgets as a household would," says Stephanie Kelton, one of MMT's leading economists. "They can use their currency-issuing capacity to pursue policies aimed at maintaining a full employment economy."[3] MMT promoters insist they are merely describing how government money works and deducing the policies that logically follow from it.

Part of the theory's appeal rested on facts that anyone can see. For instance, the U.S. Federal Reserve can simply buy bonds, that is, "print money," indefinitely as an easy way to juice the stock market—which indeed it did almost continuously from 2008 to 2022. Moreover, for most of that period it was able do so without the slightest hint of inflation. This flew in the face of the budgetary dogmas of neoclassical economists and deficit hawk politicians, who axiomatically believe that deficit spending by governments will accelerate inflation by devaluing the currency and driving up prices.[4] Yet for well over a decade the balance sheet of the Federal Reserve steadily expanded, through all of its various monetary stimulus programs, by $8 trillion.[5] In response to the COVID-19 pandemic in early 2020, the Fed intervened in global credit markets with an unprecedented pledge, if necessary, to flood the markets with a deluge of dollars three times as large, some $23.5 trillion.[6] In effect, MMT provided a formal theory for the post-2008, de facto state policy of unlimited monetary expansion, as the central banks flooded private banks and corporations with tidal waves of free money, like some gigantic iron lung pumping oxygen into the comatose body of a braindead patient.[7] If the British aristocrat Keynes was writing at the twilight of the British Empire, the MMT movement emerged in the darkening glow of another senescent superpower, offering similar remedies to stay the terminal decline of American capitalism.

Reversals

MMT believers initially appeared vindicated by the U.S. government's response to the COVID-19 depression. While the vast majority of government relief flowed directly into corporate bank accounts—$8.8 trillion, tallying up legislative and Federal Reserve actions—about a fifth of it was reserved for assisting ordinary people.[8] As $1.8 trillion of emergency stimulus was pumped into the economy in the heat of the moment and without concern for inflationary consequences, the economy began to recover. It appeared that robust, assertive fiscal policies were back in a big way, but it did not last long. Soon enough, an imbalance between government-fueled domestic demand and the pandemic's disruptions to global supply chains would set off an inflationary wave that engulfed high- and middle-income countries across every continent. In early 2022, the Russian invasion of Ukraine worsened the problem, exacerbating core inflation in food and energy prices.

After a forty-year absence, soaring prices of products and services have become a major problem again for the first time since the late 1970s. Combined with a restive workforce emboldened by favorable labor market conditions, monetary officials have dusted off the old crisis-fighting playbook of Paul Volcker, the Fed chair who famously pushed interest rates high enough to trigger a savage worldwide depression in the early 1980s that at once tamed inflation, disciplined uppity workers, and devastated the indebted countries of the Third World. Now MMT appears decisively discredited in the eyes of its critics, as the very thing MMT economists said would not happen, happened. With the current Fed chair Jerome Powell invoking the ghost of Volcker, raising interest rates while scaling down its bond-buying program, the U.S. government prepares to pull the plug from the iron lung, risking a recession to save capitalism once again by throwing millions into workless misery.

Simply put, MMT's moment came to an end because it fell out of sync with the prerogatives of power. Nearly two decades of low interest rates and the needs of government crisis management made it seem as if it accurately described what money is and how it works, opening the possibility for a return to a broadly social democratic fiscal policy. But as soon as the U.S. government shifted into a much tighter monetary policy it quickly ceased to apply. Despite its insistence that it only offers an accurate description of how money works, its irrelevance in the light of changing conditions is due to the fact that MMT, like most Keynesian theory, ignores the class basis for actually existing monetary policies, for why state actors do what they do.

Central banks, especially the Fed, are not interested in the implications of monetary sovereignty, much less in reducing inequality. Nor do they care much about new theories claiming to prove the feasibility of social democratic spending programs. They basically care about one thing: preserving "price stability," which for Fed Chair Powell is "the bedrock of our economy."[9] While the conventional story is about trimming down demand to match supply, the overriding aim of U.S. central bank policy is to maintain the value of assets priced in the dollar. These assets include about half of all internationally traded bonds and 60 percent of the world's foreign exchange reserves held by other central banks.[10] It also includes the value of stocks held in that currency, around $40 trillion traded on U.S. exchanges, which represent most of the world's publicly traded stock. Rising inflation depresses the dollar's value in relation to other currencies, devaluing these investments. In short, inflation past a certain point is intolerable for the owners of the world's wealth, as it cuts into stock prices, interest payments collected on loans issued by banks, and the value of investments in bonds— including the most important bonds of all, U.S. Treasury bonds. In a country like the USA, in which some 80 percent of GDP is made up of the labor-intensive services sector, inducing a recession to remove pressures from the labor market appeared as the most direct way to restore price stability, regardless of the fact that workers' incomes—modestly rising after decades of staying flat— crept up at a rate well below the rise in prices.[11] For the Wall Street bankers who run U.S. monetary policy the necessary course of action is obvious.

Across the recent periods of both low and high inflation, the purpose of U.S. monetary policy remained the same: to prop up the asset values of a transnational class of owners, a complacent mob of lumpen billionaires who can no longer generate the capital investment necessary to sustain global growth. The social power of this class stems from their control over the laboring lives of billions of people, a form of control mediated by money. Governments intervene in the monetary system so that economic growth can proceed through reproducing this class relationship. Paradoxically, the notion of monetary sovereignty rose to popularity because a steady flow of government money was necessary to keep growth at an acceptable level during the long slump following the financial crisis of 2008. That is, it was precisely the tightening constraints and narrowing options a slowing world economy imposed on national states, their dwindling "sovereignty," that made monetary sovereignty plausible as an idea. At the same time, these policies did not address the underlying recessionary tendencies that made them necessary in the first place, amounting to a short-term palliative that kept the global economy afloat by locking in the structural conditions for a low-investment, low-growth domestic economy.[12] "Policymakers" are consigned to making policies whose main purpose is not to help anyone, but merely to keep a sputtering system on life support. In this context, trying to persuade a caste of technocrats to guide the economy in a more humane direction is futile. Like Kafka's K., it projects an illusion of rational authority onto officials who are, at best, the bewildered custodians of an order they do not fully understand.

From MMT to Neo-Chartalism

So much, then, for MMT's rise and rapid fall from grace. Still, taking a closer look at how the theory imagines money can open up a deeper understanding of politics, money, and the state. For a time MMT may have described existing monetary policy, but it is not reducible to it. Claiming to be a general theory of money, it reverses much of the received wisdom in economics. In one of economists' most venerable folktales, money naturally emerged from the inconveniences of barter. As people trade with one another, they face the problem that they can only exchange with the particular goods they happen to have, so that if two people want to trade, each has to have something the other wants. Money simplifies the process by serving as something that everyone values and anyone will accept for payment.

This idyllic scene of private agents exchanging goods and services with one another to satisfy their wants is the real basis of economic life, according to the predominant, neoclassical school of economics. Here, money only greases the gears of exchange, which are what really matter—to use an old neoclassical canard, it is a "neutral veil" over the real relationships of the market.[13] If left to itself, the market mechanism will lead to the mutual benefit of all parties involved, as trade continues until each individual's preferences are satisfied as much as they can be with existing resources.

MMT stands the neoclassical account of money and markets on its head. Instead of originating in private exchange, money comes from governments. Paraphrasing Keynes, Randall Wray states that

> for the past 4,000 years . . . our monetary system has been a "state money system." To simplify, that is one in which the state chooses the money of account, imposes obligations (taxes, tributes, tithes, fines, and fees) denominated in that

money unit, and issues a currency accepted in payment of those obligations.[14]

Following Keynes's *Treatise on Money*, Wray and other MMT economists see money not as a particular commodity, but first and foremost as an accounting device chosen by the public authority, which it then issues as its own liability. The currency is then accepted by buyers and sellers because, at the end of the day, they must use it to pay what they owe to the state. This sequence reverses the causal priority: it is not markets that make money, but state money that makes markets.

With this redefinition of money, MMT then draws out further reversals of orthodoxy. Rather than taxing in order to spend, governments spend money into the economy first, and only tax or borrow later to adjust prices. They can do this because, unlike you and me, they issue currencies in high demand. For instance, the U.S. government, as the sole issuer of one of the key global reserve currencies, the dollar, need only credit the bank accounts of federal contractors by instructing its central bank, the Federal Reserve, to do so. The government does not need to take money from a pre-existing stash of tax revenue, because it has the power to create the money in the first place that is then, later, collected as taxes. It is merely an accounting exercise. Likewise, when a central bank like the Fed buys bonds from banks and businesses, it does so by expanding its own balance sheet—effectively creating money on the spot through keystrokes, to use a favored MMT image. Commenting on this procedure, former Fed chair Ben Bernanke captured the formidable technical skill of elite policymakers: "We just use the computer to mark up the size of the accounts."[15]

These macroeconomic ideas are not just a legacy of MMT's Keynesian assumptions. Giving the state analytical priority in the theory of money preceded Keynes's most influential arguments by some thirty years, appearing in Germany in the early twentieth century under the heading of "chartalism." Chartalism, from the Latin *charta* meaning a token or ticket, locates the origins of money in political order. The sovereign is always responsible for legally and institutionally designing money, for shaping how it works, whom it serves, and the rules that govern its circulation through the polity—money is always a "constitutional project," in Christine Desan's formulation.[16] MMT presents itself as a continuation of chartalism. "MMT rejects the ahistorical barter narrative," Kelton explains, "drawing instead on an extensive body of scholarship known as chartalism, which shows that taxes were the vehicle that allowed ancient rulers and early nation-states to introduce their own currencies, which only later circulated as a medium of exchange among private individuals."[17] It might seem strange that a doctrine with "modern" in its name would ground itself in a theory supposedly just as true for the Sumerian kings of old as for today's United States. But while rulers may have indeed issued money in their chosen unit of account for millennia, the elaboration of this historical fact into an official philosophy of money is specifically modern.

State of Nature

The term "chartalism" was coined in 1905 by Georg Friedrich Knapp, an economist and statistician of Imperial Germany and one of the chief ancestors of MMT, when he published *The State Theory of Money*.[18] Written in the twilight of the classical international gold standard, Knapp's theory took direct aim at metallic notions of money, or "metallism," which identified the essence of money with the physical properties of the precious metals. He argued that the conventional definition of money as a medium of exchange is only a special case of the more general concept of the means of payment, the officially accepted unit for settling debts, which can take forms that may or may not involve a metal base.

With its analysis of the monetary system as a legally constructed "administrative phenomenon," *The State Theory* was an intellectual expression of German *dirigisme* around the turn of the twentieth century, the governmental project actively to organize the national economy into a more competitive shape by leveling industrial tariffs (mainly against Great Britain), forming cartels across its heavy industries and banking sector, and carefully managing the exchange rate of the Deutschmark— again, primarily against the British pound.[19] Chartalism is thus a useful philosophy for underwriting projects of economic statecraft.[20] While Knapp declares in the first sentence of the book that "money is a creature of law," he later clarifies that the state "is not, in fact, bound by its laws, which it only maintains for its subjects: from time to time it of itself creates new rights and obligations to meet the facts administratively, and perhaps afterward changes the law to make it correspond."[21] Laws do not determine what is to count as money, "for they are powerless against their creator, the State; the state in its payments decides what is . . . money and the Law Courts follow suit."[22] The state is as a demiurge, creating and destroying through acts of its will.[23] Neoclassicals assume the individual, bartering trader as their most basic unit; chartalism takes the state as the foundational concept of economic life. It effectively opposes the methodological individualism of the neoclassicals with methodological statism, swapping one transhistorical assumption with another.

In the *State Theory*, money changes historically, but the state as its generative principle stands outside history, designating and modifying the currency as necessary to "meet the facts." It is quite literally naturalized. Like many economists of the time, Knapp was heavily influenced by classical mechanics, but particularly by the ideas of the French mathematician Jean-Louis Lagrange, who sought to model the movements of physical systems in a small set of elegant equations. In fact, *The State*

Theory has been described by one of Knapp's foremost students as an explicit attempt to "apply the Lagrangian principle to the essence of money: the constitution of a complex system in a simple formulation."[24] One of its strangest features is its baroque terminology, a catalogue of Greek and Latin neologisms that, according to the author, are meant to give it the aura of an empirical science, like chemistry or botany.[25] These terms, which Knapp enthusiastically proclaims to be "founded upon Political Science," mimic the Latinate names of zoological and botanical species with words like *valuta*, *hylodromy*, and *authylism*. The text composes a natural history of the monetary system, a taxonomy that classifies the many appearances of money into their most basic elements. As the origin of monetary species, the state literally becomes a force of nature.

The metaphor is not incidental to his argument. Knapp was part of an intellectual and political movement in fin-de-siècle Germany, a group of academic reformers who came together to form the Verein für Sozialpolitik (the Association for Social Policy). The Verein was formed by a cadre of historians, statisticians, and economists seeking a scientific solution to the escalating intensity of class conflict in Germany around the turn of the century. They were liberal reformers alarmed by the rapid growth of an extraordinarily wealthy money class at the top, and an increasingly assertive, openly revolutionary working class at the bottom, leaving a squeezed, embattled middle stratum (*Mittelstand*) caught between them.[26] Knapp and his colleagues, including the famous sociologist Max Weber and the influential economic historian Gustav Schmoller, sought to provide the basis for a science of reform that could resolve the antagonisms emerging with Germany's transformation into a rapidly urbanizing, industrializing society, enabling it to compete effectively with its Great Power rivals. At its core, this meant the development of a scientifically trained government capable of placing the "general interest" before the particular, narrow interests of any given class. This was a vision for the moral unity of the nation, to be achieved through reforms based on scientific research and carried out through the impartial, systematic administration of the state.[27] In Knapp's own formulation, this held out the possibility that the German Empire, as a meritocratic bureaucracy (*ein Beamtenstaat*), "could probably be the first to overcome the confusions and errors of the economic class struggle."[28]

For Knapp and the Verein, it was the very discipline imposed on states by the working class and the world market that makes "objective," scientific administration necessary in the first place. In contrast to his neo-chartalist epigones who see monetary engineering as part of a recipe for democratic politics, the founder of chartalism clearly recognized the class antagonisms and geo-political pressures *behind* the need for the state to enact chartalist policies. In a historical period much like our own marked by creeping legitimacy crises, slow-motion economic collapse, and escalating struggles in the streets, the governing caste had to manipulate money to raise national competitiveness and redirect internal antagonisms pushing toward domestic breakdown outward, venting them into the external space of geopolitics.

Thus, Knapp's abstraction of monetary governance into a realm above law and democracy reflects a basic contradiction of the nation state, riven between its existence as a national "community" of citizens, whose supposed common interest is the source of its political legitimacy, and its nature as a class state, its organization by the schism between a propertied, rich elite and the immiserated masses they rule. Scientific administration emerges as an intellectual and institutional form of class rule that must strive endlessly to reconcile this contradiction. As part of this effort, monetary policies are means by which competing nation states wage commercial warfare to capture the profits extracted from the world working class. Fueled by profits, economic growth can effectively conceal the class nature of the state, reinforcing the myth of the "national interest." Conversely, its slowing typically exposes the reality of the nation state as an organized form of economic domination. Law and money are not tools, neutral in themselves, that can be manipulated for different political interests. As forms of governance, they are inevitably class weapons, precisely because they are wielded in the name of the general interest.

Assume a Banker

Keynes was enthusiastic about Knapp's argument, citing it approvingly in the first chapter of his *Treatise on Money*. This is unsurprising, as Knapp's social and economic thought brings together most of what Geoff Mann defines as the Keynesian critique.[29] Here, "Keynesianism" means more than its conventional depiction as an economics of public works and full employment. It is a renovation of liberalism, an immanent critique of liberal philosophy and governance that recurs, appearing and reappearing in periods of upheaval when the traditional laissez-faire rulebook must be thrown out to make room for urgent action in the present, not in the make-believe world of economics textbooks but in the world in which we actually live. For this task, "Keynesian reason points to the *centrality of centrality*: to the political function of the state as the sole, if flawed, legitimate universal institution."[30] Governments, from the Keynesian point of view, are capable of dissolving social conflicts through the scientific rule of a techno-philosophical elite, who see through the clash of competing interests to govern in the general interest. The management of money is critical to this project.

For Keynes, money is in essence a temporal phenomenon. As he put it in the *General Theory*, "The importance of money essentially flows from its being a link between the present and future."[31] Money is the locus of conflicting notions about what the future holds, which translate into different attitudes toward investment in the present; conversely, unforeseen events in the present affect ideas about the future. Money and investment are psychologically driven, the object of fluctuating optimism and pessimism in the state of investors' long-term expectations about an uncertain future. And so it falls to governments to step in and act when investors, out of excessive caution or uncertainty, will not invest enough to meet the needs of society. If responsible public authorities use fiscal and monetary policy to induce such investment, then money can operate in a way that benefits the whole society, rather than just a privileged group of wealthy rentiers. The Keynesian faith in money as a technical instrument reflects the belief in a class-neutral state ideally directed by scientific experts who look out for the common good.

This faith is shared among contemporary Keynesians, including the promoters of MMT, in the claim that money is essentially a unit of account—a promise to pay, or IOU. Against monetarism, which simplistically fixates on the money supply (bank reserves) as the basis for new loans, the Keynesian argument runs the other way, focusing on the fact that bank credit creates new money. Banks issue loans, interest-earning assets on one side of their balance sheets, by creating deposits, which they record as liabilities to the borrower on the other side. Of course, the question becomes what counts as real money when debts come due. Keynesian theory—reflecting the current practice of central banks—recognizes a built-in hierarchy of money. Some forms of "money" are more acceptable than others to pay a debt. During a boom, for instance, many different forms of credit can circulate and function as means of payment, but when the bust hits, they can be abruptly devalued to the point of worthlessness, triggering a scramble for safety. And in the hierarchy that structures the world monetary system, u.s. dollars (u.s. state debt) sit at the top as the safest assets available. This is the practical basis for the concept of monetary sovereignty.

This credit-based notion of money is a serviceable description of the monetary system. It accurately describes the "world in which we actually live," as Keynes would put it, since it adds up to an abstract model of the accounting and management techniques practiced by government officials and private bankers as they manage their funding needs through a turbulent, global money market.[32] Like all economic theory, it is built on the practical consciousness of market agents themselves. But this feature marks its limits. Although articulated from the standpoint of the modern nation state, Keynesian analysis is based on a theory of the psychology of market actors. It does not try to explain that psychology, but presupposes it as data for governments to manipulate in the name of the general interest. This conceptualization obscures the process through which economic crises transform the relationship between markets and states, and the relation of money to both, in the historical evolution of the capitalist economy. That is, it obscures the deeper forces that ultimately determine the self-understanding of both market *and* state actors, the habits of investors and the mentality of government experts alike. As a managerial discourse from the point of view of the state, Keynesian theory rules out a critical analysis *of* the state itself. This is why it tends to boil down, in practice, to a defense or rationalization of what government officials are already doing. All of this points to the need not for a state theory of money, but for a money theory of the state.

Money and Time

Keynes was right: money is a temporal phenomenon, but not in the way he thought, or at least not at its deepest level. Pick a typical product of contemporary globalization—say, a laptop computer. A laptop is sold for money by the company that owns it only as the end result of a transnational sequence of extraction, processing, manufacturing, assembly, transportation, and distribution, involving thousands of laborers doing different kinds of work for a range of contractors across dozens of countries. These companies vie with one another to offer the most competitive terms by ramping up the productivity of their workers, producing more in less time than their competitors; and they, in turn, will engage their own contractors who will do the same. The tech firm selling the final product, for example, Apple, also pushes its employees to the point of burnout.[33] It will also issue bonds to raise cash and invest in financial products to insure against the risks associated with every part of this supply chain, including the political risks associated with worker unrest. In this way, it acts much like a bank, arranging its balance sheet in a way that best allows it to profitably fund its investments.[34] But the goal for Apple, its contractors, and their competitors is always the same: when everything is tabulated, to have more dollars at the end of the day than at the beginning.

Though it will involve different arrangements from case to case, the same is true for every corporation in the world. Corporate balance sheets do not just record the movement of market prices; they indirectly trace the accumulated, con-centrated time of innumerable human efforts transmuted into the common form of money. Money, accordingly, becomes their universal equivalent, a shared standard by which their value is measured. This role is currently played by the u.s. dollar.

In this system, what individual businesses experience as the competitive pressure for profit is a result of a system-wide drive to raise productivity, regardless of the bounds of the market—the key dynamic of capitalist production. From the standpoint of the owners of capital, this effectively reduces all the diverse forms of labor to the same measure: comparable, compressible expenditures of time. Yet by imposing this reduction on labor and constantly pushing to produce more in less time, capital sears coercion, violence, stupefaction, and hostility, the raw materials of class conflict, into the core of money itself. The blind pursuit of money by banks and businesses is only the flip side of this systemic, relentless drive for higher productivity and the social antagonisms it engenders.[35]

As a universal equivalent, money becomes a measure of time, the way the system evaluates, regulates, and disciplines everything from the different kinds of work people do to the temporal pressures of everyday life. As such, "money" names an alienated form of power: relationships between human beings that take on an impersonal existence independent of its creators and in turn dominate them. To everyday perception, as well as in the theoretical elaborations of everyday perception that make up economics, money appears to represent different things, like market relationships, material goods and services, or state authority. Actually, the reverse is the case: these things now represent money as an autonomous power, which invests them all with its sovereign aura.

Through this reversal, or fetishism, which makes money seem to be valuable for its own sake, material resources are produced and distributed only as incidental byproducts of the limitless drive for money. Money does not conveniently exist to circulate goods and services, but is the reason goods and services exist in the first place. It is a means that becomes its own end, which is still only a means—a contradiction rooted in the class relations of commodity production.

Money regulates the social organization of time. It co-ordinates the productive life of society, but from behind the backs of the producers, the workers of the world who form an interconnected, interdependent association of thickening density—the planetary laborer. Debt-enserfed American students compete for a shrinking number of jobs on laptops assembled by Chinese manufacturing workers in Shenzen, whose computer chips are manufactured by factory workers in Taipei, the metal and minerals for which are extracted under brutal conditions by cobalt and lithium miners in the Democratic Republic of Congo and Chile, perhaps with the completed product transported on container ships run by Danish sailors supplied with wheat harvested by Russian farmers. The profits produced by this planetary assemblage are the excess time of human association extracted by the transnational capitalist class, the top 1 percent who owns nearly half the world's wealth.[36] We all work longer and harder than we need to not for any collective purpose, but so that this class can continue to get richer.

Money did not, and does not, enable this planet-spanning productive formation. Rather, it is itself the result of a process of reconfiguration that occurred outside of any state actor's conscious intent. As the global division of labor has become transnationally integrated through value chains and logistics channels; as work itself has become increasingly molded by its dependence upon the whims of the stock exchange and the broader financial markets, themselves dependent on the continued largess of the central banks; as the reproduction of the basic social relations through which material goods are provided becomes ever more dependent on this gargantuan monetary edifice; and as the experience of labor, paradoxically, grows more fragmented, precarious, and uncertain, the more a world market for labor comes into existence—in short, the more transnational social labor becomes, the more money becomes world money, its equally transnational representation.

The Architecture of World Money

World money serves as the most widely used and accepted currency in the global economy. Consider the u.s. dollar, the currency at the top of the world monetary hierarchy. The dollar makes up 60 percent of global currency reserves and is involved in 90 percent of foreign exchange trading.[37] It is the unit of account for invoicing most of world trade, for pricing key commodities, like oil, and for nearly half of a $544 trillion global derivatives market.

Its central position makes it the most desired currency in the world, a universally accepted store of value, unit of account, and means of payment for international transactions, credit creation, securitization, and flows of funds. This is somewhat peculiar, though. While the u.s. share of world trade, the economic weight behind the dollar, has steadily eroded over the last several decades, the dollar remains the world's premier currency.[38] How is it possible to sustain this tension? For an answer, we need to look at the dollar's role as a means of payment, particularly its use in the international market for u.s. state debt.

When the u.s. government "prints money," it buys bonds and other assets from banks, corporations, and a small class of rich asset owners, replacing their securities with cash; likewise, when it "borrows," it issues Treasury debt to the private market, where it then circulates as a safe, guaranteed asset for investors—some $22 trillion worth, as of early 2023.[39] This debt base, in turn, fuels further credit creation, as both banks and businesses that are not technically banks but act like them—asset managers like hedge funds, for instance—can borrow against their holdings of Treasury debt to fund their investments. Essentially, both make money by borrowing it at a lower rate of interest than the rate at which they lend, some of which provides funding to non-financial corporations by investing in their stocks and bonds. The world market in money and capital in which all of this occurs is sometimes referred to as the "shadow banking system," since much of the borrowing and lending within it goes on with little to no government oversight. This unregulated, unmonitored agglomeration of private equity funds, mutual funds, insurance companies, pension funds, bank-spawned legal entities ("special purpose vehicles") and a host of other shady outfits are the cauldron of world credit creation.[40] As "the financial mirror image of larger underlying trends of economic inequality," its total size has grown exponentially over the last two decades, now holding some $183 trillion or 49 percent of the world's financial assets. At

212 percent of global GDP, this dwarfs the balance sheets of even the biggest banks.[41] Little wonder it is the shadow banking sector that is financing the bulk of the recent, record-breaking rise of corporate debt, which reached an all-time high in 2019.

A steady flow of trustworthy state debt, especially U.S. Treasury debt, is critical to the world financial market because it is treated as the safest asset in the system—everyone assumes the U.S. government will continue to pay the interest on its debts. This virtual guarantee allows it to act as widely accepted collateral for businesses to secure the loans they need to fund their activities and service their debts. Or, to put it another way, government bonds can easily be traded for cash because there will usually be buyers ready to take it. There is thus a tight link between state debt and liquidity, or the option easily to convert a security into its cash equivalent with no change in price. Liquidity is the circulating blood in the veins of the global financial system. Without it, markets cannot be made, prices cannot be formed, no one can sell what they need without huge losses, sending the entire system into a sort of heart attack—a liquidity crisis. To prevent this from happening, states are compelled to manufacture liquidity by issuing bonds to be used as premium collateral for borrowing and lending, mainly through a deceptively simple legal instrument called the repurchase agreement, or "repo."[42] Repo is the legal form that most funding, and thus liquidity, takes in the world money market. It is basically a lending agreement through which a borrower obtains funds by selling a bond that it agrees to buy back for a higher price after a short period, sometimes just overnight. Central banks use repo operations constantly to adjust the money supply by selling and buying bonds in the open market. Standing repo trades finance more than $12 trillion, 75 percent of which is based on government collateral, thus playing an instrumental role in making the global market for U.S. Treasury bonds.[43] State debt, shadow banking, and repo contracts make up the dark architecture of contemporary world money.

Shadow banking is the volatile core of the world financial system, and the state debt–repo relation is at the center of it. As Daniela Gabor observes, "sovereign debt has become the cornerstone of modern financial systems, used as a benchmark for pricing assets, to hedge positions in fixed income markets, and as collateral for credit creation via shadow banking."[44] Government debt is required as repo collateral in two-thirds of both the u.s. and European debt markets, which are the largest in the world. Consequently, "the state has become a collateral factory for shadow banking, and for big banks' activities in the shadows."[45] For currencies like the dollar or the euro to serve as reserve money for the global economy, to function as a universal means of exchange and payment, a dominant unit of account, a measure and store of value—in short, to serve as world money—governments must put their fiscal and monetary policies at the service of international money markets whose activities they do not supervise, much less control. As collateral factories, they have little choice but to keep pumping out the debt that keeps the entire system running even as its overall growth indicators steadily tick down, year by year.

Centralizing Disintegration

Since the watershed of 2008 the Federal Reserve has become a kind of "lender of last resort" for the dollar-based global economy, swelling its balance sheet through asset purchases to nearly $9 trillion from just under $1 trillion in 2007. The Fed's further expansion of its balance sheet in 2020 fed a binge of corporate borrowing that led to a full 20 percent of the 3,000 largest American companies no longer earning enough to pay their interest expenses, mutating into "zombie companies," de facto wards of the state.[46] However, 2020 only solidified an already existing trend, which was well in place for decades prior to the COVID-19 pandemic —corporate zombification has been rising since the late 1980s.[47]

The other major central banks of the G10 countries have followed a similar pattern, with the tab of total commitments to monetary stimulus standing somewhere around $15 trillion.[48] This amounted to nearly one-fifth of the entire global economy in 2019.[49] The balance sheets of the Federal Reserve and the European Central Bank both total between 45 and 50 percent of annual GDP of the United States and the Eurozone, respectively. Expanding central bank accounts through stimulus and asset purchases is complemented by the expansion of state debt, as discussed in the last section. State debt, especially U.S. debt, has been steadily rising since the early 1980s, but since 2008 it has been rising exponentially. At $27 trillion, U.S. federal debt stands at almost 130 percent of GDP; in the Eurozone, total sovereign debt is 95 percent of EU GDP.[50]

The flood of U.S. and European debt marks a worldwide trend. Japan's state debt is currently at 230 percent of GDP, while China's domestic (non-foreign) debt is over 300 percent of GDP.[51] Taking the 37 countries of the OECD area, by the end of 2019 sovereign debt had expanded to 72 percent of total GDP, feeding a huge buildup in non-financial corporate debt, the heart of the so-called real economy of production and investment, which reached a record high of $13.5 trillion in the same year.[52] Overall global debt-to-GDP was already over 300 percent before the onset of the coronavirus pandemic in the first quarter of 2020.[53]

The most striking development, however, is not the absolute debt levels themselves, but the sclerotic production system this mountain of debt is piled upon. Across the capitalist world, pre-pandemic 2019 was already one of the most dismal years for productivity growth in recent memory, again dashing hopes that, finally, the world economy would bounce back from the nadir of the Great Recession.[54] In fact, business profits were back at recession levels, trending downward to the low point of a decade before.[55] Contemporary investment, when it does provide jobs, mainly provides low-wage, low-productivity work which, in the

OECD area, indeed makes up the vast majority of what new work has been created since 2008. The anemic level and inferior quality of investment underlies the well-documented, decades-long trend of flat or falling wages for workers, whose share of income has continued to decline over the last fifteen years.[56] The great mass of that income flowed into capital gains, basically rents, for the owners of financial assets, helped along by a delirious rally in asset prices stoked by unlimited central bank stimulus. This trifecta of decaying growth, widening inequality, and exploding state debt is transnational, affecting virtually every country producing for the world market.[57] But beneath the indicators as their common source is stagnating systemic productivity, appearing in a steady stream of graphs and charts like an electroencephalogram showing at once the fading vital signs of a terminal social order and the flatlining mental abilities of the rulers responsible for it.

During the COVID-19 pandemic a brief uptick in labor productivity growth was the cause for some excitement among economic commentators. A "productivity boom" could be at hand, enthused the *Washington Post*, quoting economists who were optimistic that the pandemic would trigger innovations in artificial intelligence and robotics that would boost productivity for years to come.[58] It looked, finally, as if the long malaise of declining productivity might finally have lifted, allowing the economy to resume robust rates of growth that could power widespread prosperity. Alas, the uptick had a more banal origin. It was only a mirage created by the pandemic's impact on the labor market: total hours worked declined far more quickly than total GDP, as millions of people were thrown out of work by the pandemic while the economy was aided by temporary government stimulus—fewer workers with similar GDP made it look, in the statistics, like labor productivity was improving. But far from kicking off a productivity boom the economy quickly reverted to trend. According to the Conference Board, an international organization that tracks global productivity trends, world labor productivity has bottomed out and is expected to remain basically non-existent for the foreseeable future.[59] These trends lead the organization to conclude that overall global growth will not only revert to prepandemic levels, which were already pathetic, but "are likely to be below the prepandemic trend."[60] All of this indicates that the pursuit of greater productivity through capital investment, the engine of capitalist growth, has stalled out, and shows no signs of coming back.

Global productivity growth appears to be over for the foreseeable future. The result is likely to be a kind of stasis state in which national governments must take ever more extreme measures to compensate for the paralysis of private capitalism. As growth stalls out, the system's instability becomes more severe, continuing to detonate crises that governments, especially the government with the most important currency, the USA, must continue to try to stabilize however they can through monetary policies. This is where the contradiction between the state's role as the general custodian of capital and the supervisor of the general interest of its citizens becomes unavoidable. As one example, the Federal Reserve's crusade to lower inflation risks a severe recession that would undermine the government's own efforts to revive the U.S. economy through a new industrial policy. Yet the central bank must be allowed to act independently, regardless of the damage it inflicts on U.S. society and the world, because it must remain a responsible steward of the monetary system in the eyes of the world's dollar investors. Policy incoherence of this kind is a result of the fact that the "monetary sovereign" does not fully control its own currency as world money, but remains subordinated to it, condemned to serve its own creation.

Globally, the ever-tighter fusion between state institutions and private financial markets, and the political fission of nationalist reaction it feeds, is the core of a process of centralizing disintegration. The more money evolves into a centralized, governmental instrument of global crisis management, the more it is accompanied by a parallel return of the fragmenting politics of space and place: nostalgia for a lost, better past, the basic fantasy that fuels every form of communitarian nationalism. It is a fantasy because it is hopeless: national policies cannot address the transnational origins of the system's breakdown. But the tightening constraints imposed by the need to keep a dying system on life support feeds an overwhelming sense of helplessness that sustains a boom in visions of national liberation. In the United States, ethnonationalists dream of a white reich, Christian nationalists of the millenarian purification of a nation steeped in sin; addled Internet addicts hope for a Caesarist figure (Trump was the latest) to overthrow a corrupted government, wresting American sovereignty back from a cabal of reptilian globalist conspirators; and neo-Cold Warriors see the renewal of grand ideological and strategic conflict with China as the last hope to revive a fading superpower. These are the fever dreams of an anxious age staring down a terrifyingly uncertain future, the product of decades of complacent assumptions about u.s. global supremacy evaporating before our eyes. However, u.s. decline is not the result of any foreign power undermining it from without, supernatural or otherwise. It is a result of the epochal collapse of the global liberal order made in America's own image, to which its fate is chained. Far from saving that order, the u.s. government is forced to take economic measures, particularly with regard to finance, that only hasten its demolition.

five

Endgame

A metallic deity tops a monolith of stone reaching halfway to the clouds: Ceres, the Roman goddess of harvest and fertility, shines from the summit of the temple. Her aluminum skin clashes with the building's limestone cladding even as her vertical lines echo its skyward rise. In antiquity, she guarded a lower passage between the living and the dead, the *mundus cerialis*, where her worshipers offered grains as tribute. Now, gleaming high above the Chicago Board of Trade, she looms rectilinear, impassive, and austere, a distinctly modern idol. Symbolizing the grain trade central to Chicago's commercial history, she could also be a patroness of alchemy: the original derivatives market emerged here with the founding of the Board's futures exchange in 1848, made possible by diluvial flows of wheat, the product of Midwestern farmers, streaming into the city. In the late twentieth century, the Board would host innovations in derivative finance that eventually conquered the world.

Today, Ceres keeps her vigil above an altered passage to the lower realms. The Board's trading pits, once filled with human voices, are now silent except for the hum of computers—a strange, modern *mundus cerialis* beneath a citadel of finance. The goddess now guards a doorway to the afterlife of production, where the fading growth of the capitalist economy appears in the rising numbers flashing across the screens of automated trading platforms.

The Latest Search for Order

We live in an interregnum between a dying regime and some unknown successor. The Great Financial Crisis of 2008 destroyed the credibility and confidence of what had been the neoliberal model of financial government, shattering the illusions of an entire generation of technocrats. For several decades u.s. economic officials had assumed that a hands-off policy approach would allow markets to operate correctly. If they just remained free from governmental interference, the story went, banks and other financial institutions would allocate resources efficiently throughout the economy, ensuring prosperity for everyone. Independent central banks would maintain the stability of prices by making fine-tuned adjustments to key interest rates. Raising rates would cut back on borrowing, slowing the economy down; lowering them would prompt more investment by encouraging more lending. Monetary policy could ensure that economies remained at equilibrium, with employment neither declining enough to threaten social instability, nor rising so high as to threaten inflation. In this finely orchestrated dance, market distortions would be marginal or non-existent, since prices supposedly reflected all available information. All that was required was a steady hand with a light touch. In practice, this meant leaving it to the enlightened central bankers, most memorably personified by the Ayn Rand disciple Alan Greenspan. Greenspan's sophomoric fables about market efficiency earned him the sobriquet "The Maestro" on Wall Street.

The great meltdown of 2008 and its grinding, interminable aftermath put paid to these comforting laissez-faire notions. Since then, over a decade of new financial regulations and experimental monetary policies has not dispelled a malaise of stagnation in the u.s. economy. They have certainly helped to juice corporate profits to record highs, fueling an ongoing bonanza of stock buybacks, downsizing, dividend payments, and speculative trading in financial markets.[1] As pointed out in the previous chapter, u.s. corporations also benefit from their position at the top of a global network of value chains from which they extract the bulk of the profit produced through them, while at home they enjoy a favorable business environment thanks to a forty-year assault on the living standards of the people who work for them, led with alacrity by the u.s. government itself. But none of this has been enough to spur broad-based growth, or help the rates of business investment it depends on.[2] Looking a little closer at the profit data themselves gives a clue as to why: as recent research has shown, lower corporate taxes (essentially a redistribution of income from workers to business owners) and low interest rates (which make it easy to borrow and invest in financial markets) are responsible for a full one-third of all profit growth among s&p 500 companies since 2004.[3] u.s. corporations are clearly dependent on state support to sustain profitability, but this does not lead to greater investment.

Far from being confined to the usa, the investment slowdown is a worldwide trend. Before the covid-19 pandemic, the world economy was already descending into recession, led by a steady deterioration in GDP growth in the high-income countries since 2010.[4] As the pandemic hit, it kicked off a frenzy of emergency government spending in countries where, to take the G7 as a sample, such spending already counted for between 38 and 50 percent of GDP.[5] In the United States, government expenditure has been steadily rising as a proportion of GDP since the middle of the twentieth century, making up 42 percent of it as of early 2023.[6] Still the recovery never fully arrives, despite official voices constantly reassuring us that it is just around the corner. A certain mood for perestroika has settled over America's best and brightest, as economists, policymakers, and their media apparatchiks search for reforms that could revive growth and once again set the system on firm foundations.

The state of economic stasis has called forth a growing chorus of calls for more vigorous fiscal responses on the part of national governments. These have come from some unusual places. The International Monetary Fund, long one of the most enthusiastic cheerleaders for neoliberal policies, has been calling for more fiscal policy since 2013. The Clintonite economist and former Secretary of the Treasury Lawrence Summers, and his fellow Harvard luminary Jason Furman, have decided in no uncertain terms that "active fiscal policy is essential in order to maximize employment and maintain financial stability."[7] When people like this invoke the notion of "fiscal policy," they usually mean investing in things like infrastructure and education, and perhaps bolstering demand through mildly progressive taxation. This view is shared by the Biden Administration's Council of Economic Advisors, who are less concerned with budget constraints than the typical economist soothsayers recruited by Democratic presidents.[8]

Further leftward, progressive economists push for more ambitious responses. In *Mission Economy*, Mariana Mazzucato calls for a return to an industrial policy based on "long-run, vision-oriented public investments" to restore broad-based and equitable growth. This would end the financial sector's ability to impose its need for short-term, speculative returns on the broader society, so that "finance serves the economy, rather than the economy serving finance."[9] Enlightened governments should move from assuming the unquestionable efficiency of unfettered markets to actively shaping them for progressive social goals; with an activist public sector, competitive capitalism can be given a new lease on life.

While the details differ, all such remedies for the present moment are variations on the classic Keynesian playbook: in the absence of a private sector willing to do the job, governments must step in with a renewed commitment actively to steer economic growth in the "real economy" of investment, productivity, and employment. If the neoliberal era was defined by the dominance of finance over society, then its successor will be defined by re-embedding financial markets in society, putting them to work for the common good. "When the capital development of a country becomes the by-product of a casino," as J. M. Keynes himself said, "the job is likely to be ill-done."[10]

That is the idea, anyway. The neo-Keynesian narrative is based on the understanding that the u.s. economy, to its detriment, has become "financialized." As the author of a highly regarded book on the topic, the sociologist Greta Krippner, describes it, "financialization" refers "to the tendency for profit-making in the economy to occur increasingly through financial channels rather than through productive activities."[11] The appalling upward redistribution of wealth to the financial elite flows from their outsized share of business profits since the 1980s, and their resulting perch at the top of the economic order. National governments therefore have the responsibility to learn from the failed experiments of neoliberalism, to de-financialize the economy in the name of the public interest. Keynesians typically project an image of wholeness, such as the public interest, or the common good, as the frame for politics. In this frame, the unspoken premise is the possibility for reviving national class collaboration between workers and capitalists, wielding the power of government to induce higher rates of private investment that will raise productivity, boost profits, and generate high-wage work across the economy. Assuming that the u.s. government could revive past patterns of class compromise to birth a new social democracy, fiscal nationalism idealizes a dead form of life to confront a radically different present.

But conjuring ghosts from the past does not help to grasp the present, much less transform it. What Keynesians imagine as the "public interest" in fact has little to do with the current practices of state actors, which treat financialization not as a problem, or as some parasitic growth to be removed from the real economy, but as the established paradigm of governance, the infrastructure of concepts and practices required for growth in present conditions. Under the pressures of a world economy in which production processes are steadily concentrated into ever fewer locations and firms, the world's workforce has nearly stopped growing, wealth is centralizing into the hands of a global class of asset owners, and the opportunities for profitable investment are drying up, the premier capitalist states have been compelled to involve themselves ever more deeply in the mechanics of the financial system.[12]

The tighter the fusion between government and finance, the more redundant private markets become as a mechanism for allocating resources, as these are gradually replaced by government financial operations. The result drives an intensifying double movement in which finance is governmentalized and government financialized, a cryptoplanning regime that dare not speak its own name. In a reversal of the fate of the Soviet Union, u.s. society undoes itself not by pursuing liberal reforms to revive a moribund planned economy, but by quietly liquidating the liberal institutions at the source of its ideological legitimacy and economic vitality, which in the end are also those of capitalism itself.

The Anatomy of Finance

The critique of financialization abstracts from production to focus on distribution. That is, it abstracts from a constantly evolving conflict over the organization and control of time, the efforts by which businesses try to compel their employees to work longer and harder for less and the countless ways that workers resist this, including attempts to exercise control over the techniques and forms of the labor process itself. The daily combat inherent in reproducing society through the capitalist relations of production has its own shifting momentum and tide of battle that reflects the balance of class forces not just at the national level, but globally. Financialization theory, and the social-democratic politics it animates, redefines all of this as a technical economic function—producing and trading commodities, as in Krippner's conventional definition. It shares this premise with financial thinking, which similarly abstracts from production to analyze economic data as various, tradable flows of funds.

The security is the basic building block of finance. What is a security? Simply, it is any tradable claim on some future stream of revenue. This rings familiar to modern ears, but some of its elements have archaic roots. Debt contracts, of course, have existed for thousands of years, as has lending at compound interest. Legal arrangements crudely resembling equity partnerships and limited liability ventures can arguably be found in the commercial activities of antiquity, particularly the private state contractors, or "publicans," of ancient Rome. During the Middle Ages, simple credit instruments like the bill of exchange were ubiquitous. These allowed merchants and bankers in both Christian and Islamic society to receive credit in exchange for the future delivery of goods or payment, creating thriving, credit-linked networks of regional trade by the twelfth century, if not earlier.[13]

A couple of centuries later, the Italian city states of the Renaissance played an outsized role in the evolutionary history of finance. Double-entry bookkeeping originated in Florence, enabling the continuation of a business concern as an impersonal, abstract concept by equating total assets with the sum of liabilities plus owners' equity—in simple terms, a business is seen as worth what it finances by issuing debt and stocks.[14] Stocks and bonds in the modern sense of these terms as tradable, interest-bearing claims of ownership in equity and debt, respectively, originated in the public banks of the Venetian and Genoese Republics, who forced their citizens to loan money to the government to fund war and commercial expansion; the citizens then formed banks with ownership shares based on what they were owed by the government, which in turn circulated as money. The first recorded joint-stock enterprise, an association of tradable share capital legally identified with the company itself, appears in the English Muscovy Company chartered in 1553, though its roots—once again—can be traced hundreds of years earlier to the monetary and legal experiments of the Genoese.[15]

Like a sprawling network of tributaries flowing into a single great river, the sources of modern finance are widely diffused over the terrain of economic, political, and legal history. But the financial security as the general form of wealth in which all property appears as revenue-generating assets, as abstract, tradable claims to a stream of payments rather than particular activities connected with specific times, places, and personalities, would only emerge with the social transformations of industrial capital in the nineteenth century. The huge outlays and long turnover times necessary for large-scale industrial investment meant a massively expanded role for banking finance, whose gradual fusion with the industrial system redefined wealth in financial terms as the ownership of assets and liabilities. But the expansion of industry also ignited a new and explosive dynamic: the incorporation of waged, unpropertied millions into mechanized mass production on an unprecedented scale.

Dragooned into the industrial labor process upon pain of starvation or imprisonment, the armies of the dispossessed made the ability to work into a political force right from the start, politicizing time itself in the fight for the eight-hour day, the five-day workweek, the slower pace of work, the general question of who controls the pace and space of laboring life. The question always arises because, as explained in Chapter Three, capitalist profits stem from unpaid labor time, or surplus value, the portion of the working day in which the worker is compelled to work for the capitalist for free. This temporal terrain of social conflict across which classes are made, unmade, and remade again is collapsed in the wage relation, wherein the worker appears simply to be paid for her labor the way any other commodity owner would be paid for her commodity. The struggle over the control of time drops out in the conception of a simple payment for a service.[16]

From the capitalist investor's perspective, labor is merely an input producing an output like any other factor of production, part of a process in which money is converted into commodities, which are then sold for more money later. This is the general circuit of capital, depicted by Marx as M-C-M'. The money capitalist is a specific type of investor who provides money for others to use in production. For this figure, money produces money in the form of interest paid by the borrower: M-M'. Interest-bearing capital, or financial income, is thus a deduction from the profits of productive investments. But for the money capitalist, it is only the flow of interest payments over time that matters. In this even more abstracted circuit of M-M', the process of production drops out entirely, leaving no trace in the mind of the financier, who, seemingly untethered to material activity, can simply advance money to receive more sometime in the future. The passing of time tout court now appears to be the source of the return. This abstraction grounds a core principle of finance, the time value of money: since it can be invested to earn a return, since interest accrues as time passes, a sum of money in hand now is always worth more than the same amount later.[17] Understood not as a construction between human beings in their concrete historical activity but as a function of money, time is automated. An extreme abstraction concealing its own basis in the circuit of capital and, at a deeper level, the wage form, the time value of money is the fetish at the heart of the modern financial security.

Stocks and bonds are the elementary forms of security that serve as the basis for a swirling kaleidoscope of secondary types:

futures, forwards, swaps, warrants, options, swaptions, CDOS (collaterized debt obligation), CDSS (credit default swaps)—a financial derivative can be designed for any occasion. Yet all derivatives, however exotic, are based on some securitized asset: an underlying source of income that has been repackaged into a tradable, legal claim on a future stream of payments. Since for investors a dollar today is worth more than a dollar tomorrow, the value of money payments received later must be adjusted, or "discounted," to reflect their value in the present. In effect, financial securities call the future into the present; they give future expectations a reality now as current prices. This is the logic of capitalization, a structural feature of securities as a type of property.

Consider a company organizing an initial public offering (IPO) of shares to become publicly traded on a stock exchange. Its original owners will have invested capital in buildings, equipment, software, materials, employee wages, and so on, but this sum could have little or nothing to do with the price its shares will fetch. This will be set by the judgement of market actors regarding the profit expectations of the business, the likely demand for its shares, its level of debt, prevailing interest rates, and so forth. If the company looks profitable and interest rates are low, its share value can be several orders of magnitude larger than the initial sum of capital, now transformed into owner's equity. A simplified example can show how this works. If the rate of interest is 5 percent and a given stock share pays a dividend of $10, the price of the share is the equivalent of $200, the amount that would be required to generate that return at that particular rate of interest, other things being equal. If the interest rate were to fall to 2 percent, the price would rise sharply to $500, as that sum invested at a 2 percent rate of return would yield $10. In practice, the calculations for any given security will be more complicated to allow for different sources of cash flow, which must each be discounted separately, but in general, the inverse relationship between interest rates and security prices will tend to hold. The prices of securities, capitalized wealth, therefore represent a fictitious form of capital, in the sense that they can represent a dramatic expansion of value purely out of expected interest payments.[18] This is the alchemy at the heart of finance.

The logic is the same with other types of securities like government bonds, only in this case there is no original invested capital, just the ability of the government to service its debts by collecting taxes or further borrowing. The interest rates on some bonds have a special role in the financial system, serving as the "risk-free rate," or the baseline return that can be earned with minimal to no risk. In the dollar-based system this role is typically filled by the interest rates on u.s. Treasury securities. Generally speaking, if the returns on a potential investment look unable to beat the risk-free rate, it is not worth pursuing; if they do, then the difference is your effective return. Returning to the above example, say you judge the stock undervalued, so you spend your $200 to buy a share. Treasuries are paying 5 percent, but you are anticipating either a rise in the stock price to at least $220, or an increase in dividends to $20. Both cases would net a nice $10 premium, or the expected return ($220) minus (discounted by) the risk-free rate ($200 at 5 percent = $210). But with this investment you have added "risk" to your assets. The stock's return is not guaranteed, while the u.s. government is nearly certain to repay its creditors. Seen in this way, the $200 can be understood as the price of taking on a certain amount of risk. Profit becomes a function of volatility, or the correlation between risk and return.

The financial security is thus a very weird thing. In the world of securities, assets become wealth through the magic of capitalization, or fictitious capital. Profit, the surplus value produced by unpaid labor and the engine of capitalist growth, becomes just another kind of capitalized revenue, no different in kind from interest, rent, or dividends—all become functions of volatility. In practice, the quantifications of finance convert the time and space of class war into a depoliticized, mathematical procedure in which profits are converted into "returns." From Chicago to Seoul, from Santiago to Yokohama, corporations in the global system of production try every day to force workers to labor harder and longer to generate enough profits for the system to sputter on. Across these same global coordinates, workers resist, withholding their labor power, striking, sabotaging, walking off the job en masse. Fueled by the desires, dreams, nightmares, and rage of hundreds of millions of people, the class struggle makes profit production into a molten terrain of permanent contestation. Capitalized assets hide the formative conflicts of the production process by representing their outcome as a calculable, predictable thing that can be treated like an algorithm. Systematic misapprehension is built into their very form.

Financial governance, then, attempts to impose order on institutions whose reproduction depends on misrecognizing the conditions of their own existence. When central banks carry out "open market operations," for example, in which they trade securities with private dealers, they aim to adjust interest rates lower or higher either to encourage or to discourage investment. To induce a healthy profit environment prices must be stable and returns attractive and predictable. Market conditions must remain liquid, or easy to trade in without major movements in the price of the assets bought and sold. In other words, the central banks share the financiers' belief that their economic existence depends only on returns on assets, divorced from their ultimate source in profits extracted through the unpredictable course of the class war. This assumption is not a mental error, but follows from the practices and policies necessary to sustain growth through financial accumulation. And the more fragile and brittle the edifice of financial accumulation becomes, the greater the pressure on the state to sustain the fetish of liquidity that keeps the whole thing turning over. This is a key way in which the leading capitalist states, especially the USA, are forced into the Sisyphean logic of trying to master capital even as they remain enslaved to it.

A Material Abstraction

Finance, in practice and theory, understands economic reality as it appears: a money-generating mechanism that has little or nothing to do with human labor. This is a curious paradox, since the origins of modern financial theory lie in an effort to model human activity in the image of the machine. This is the explicit goal of the recondite art of operations research, the foundation of the contemporary academic theory of finance. Arising during the Second World War to help the U.S. and British militaries solve logistical and coordination problems, operations research is an art of maximizing control over people and things by deploying mathematical statistics to analyze any situation as a set of predictable outcomes from initial conditions. An amalgam of industrial management, probability theory, logistics, economics, and linear programming, it aims at achieving the most efficient outcome with the minimum use of resources—or, in financial terms, maxing out returns with minimal risk. Not coincidentally, many of the first-generation figures who transformed finance into a purely calculative, analytical form of knowledge were trained in this discipline.[19]

Three fundamental propositions lay the groundwork for the grand abstraction that is the modern theory of finance. First is the claim that how corporations fund their operations, whether through issuing stock, selling bonds, or reinvesting profits, is irrelevant to the way they are valued in a perfectly competitive market—the "Modigliani Miller Theorem." One of the theorem's authors, Merton Miller, was an expert in linear programming, while his co-author, the economist Franco Modigliani, was closely involved with the Cowles Commission, a University of Chicago think tank that pioneered econometric techniques and served as a national nerve center of ops research.[20] Second, the logic by which investors should select securities to include in a portfolio can be modeled with mathematical precision as an optimal trade-off between risk and return, a line of argument inaugurated by Harry Markowitz's work on optimal portfolio selection. Markowitz conceived the idea for what eventually became known as "modern portfolio theory" in a course on ops research taught by Tjalling Koopmans, Director of the Cowles Commission from 1948 to 1955.[21] Jack Treynor and William Sharpe, both credited with independently inventing the foundation of financial theory, the Capital Asset Pricing Model (CAPM), were protegés and students of Modigliani and Markowitz, respectively.[22]

Lastly, there is the efficient markets hypothesis (EMH), famously stated by Nobel Prize winner Eugene Fama in 1970 but anticipated well before him (most importantly in the postwar period by the statistician Maurice Kendall, president of the British Operational Research Society).[23] EMH states that security prices reflect all available information and so trade at their fair market value.[24] The EMH was built on more than half a century of statistical research showing that such prices seemed to follow a "random walk," a series of unconnected movements. The series supposedly is random because, if prices are rational in reflecting all the available data, then by definition they would only change in response to wholly unexpected information. The randomness, paradoxically, is supposed to reflect the rationality of market actors.

These conceptual innovations emerged from a postwar constellation of new ideas and technologies revolving around the control of human-machine systems. Hothoused by the lavish funding and focused aims provided by the military's need for the most efficient methods of killing, scientists and engineers developed a range of powerful approaches to problems of automated control and electronics. Of course, this includes the period's most celebrated technological legacy, the computer, Alan Turing's "thinking machine," which received its first practical application in codebreaking, or cryptanalysis. The figure of the thinking machine was also central in the widely influential use of game theory in economics, whose founding is usually attributed to the polymath Cold Warrior John von Neumann. Based on his wartime work on computers, von Neumann elaborated a general theory of thinking machines, or automata, in terms of which decision-making could be theorized mathematically.

These intellectual developments underlie the emergence of operations research and its close cousin in the postwar period, systems analysis. In this algebraic world, humans become deciding machines; machines become more or less efficient versions of humans. As the historian David Noble sums it up in his brilliant social history of automation:

> in the work of operations researchers and systems analysts, social analysis, like analysis of the physical world, consisted in fracturing reality into discrete components, determining the mathematical relationships between them, and reassembling them into a new mathematically constructed whole—a "system" which now appeared to carry the force of logical necessity and thus would be amenable to formal control.[25]

The collective result was a qualitative leap in the program of scientific management, founded by Frederick Taylor half a century earlier, which analyzed the labor process and the detailed division of labor into its most fundamental components in order to reorganize them for maximum labor productivity.[26]

Indeed, control of the production process was top of mind for the owners of capital in the middle of the twentieth century. During the first half of the 1940s, the u.s. war industries were rocked by hundreds of wildcat strikes, often led by militant Black workers recently integrated into the ranks of the Congress of

Industrial Organizations.[27] Workers continued to wage war for control of the shop floor well into the postwar period, shaking core industries like automobiles to their foundations in some of the largest strike waves in u.s. history. Corporate executives complained bitterly about their loss of control. "We worked for years to eliminate chance in our operations," one lamented, "now here it comes back in a big way. A new and unpredictable element has been injected into our business."[28]

The high point of the postwar industrial workforce was to be the beginning of its decline. In the wake of one of the broadest, most sustained upsurges of labor militancy in u.s. history, operations research became an intellectual technique for waging a two-front war against Communists abroad and "subversives" at home. Intensifying, bottom-up class warfare in the 1930s and '40s had fortified industrial unions and imparted some control over the labor process to industrial workers, forcing a concrete question of power upon the managers of capital: "Who runs the shop?" On this terrain of conflict, ops research provided a method of maximizing efficiency on the shop floor by analyzing the industrial labor process into its simplest components, de-skilling the workforce, and reassembling it as a human–machine hybrid to speed up mechanization in the pursuit of greater output. Industrial applications of operations research, like the numerical control system of automated machinery, were explicitly introduced in part to undermine workers' control over the labor process. Through numerical control, formerly intricate machining techniques based on the skill and intuition of human operators could be programmed directly into the machines by managing engineers. The operators were forced to adapt to the pace and purpose of the machines, subjected to the impersonal discipline of a computer program.[29]

The dream of the automatic factory, emptied of workers but for a handful of managers and engineers, was the polestar of the postwar push for automation. Self-acting servomechanisms and feedback processes would replace living labor up to the point of maximum labor productivity, countering the "labor problem" by following what appear to be the purely technical requirements of production. Human and machine were to be dissolved into an algebraic formula, and the contradictions between mental and manual labor smoothed over, naturalized.

At the deepest level, the deletion of labor power from the theory of finance expresses capital's relentless drive to delete humans from the process of production. Its technical formulae would prove a major source of strength as deindustrialization picked up speed in the advanced capitalist world. Forged in great power conflict and refined in the class war at home, the intellectual tools of finance emerged as a "material abstraction," theory becoming a material force for managing an increasingly intricate, far-flung, transnational production system over the course of the 1970s and '80s.[30] The elegant equations of risk analysis made the global surplus manageable by rendering its sources unknowable, replacing the extraction of unpaid labor with fictitious capital values and likening the movement of market prices to the random gyrations of physical particles. Finance is nothing less than the global culmination of Taylorism as an ideology and method of control, driven by the need for capital to overcome the human barriers to its own reproduction within the industrial labor process itself.

Subtraction

Modern finance is essentially monetary Taylorism, the science of efficiency applied to the practice of making money. Like Taylorism, the native ideology of capitalist industry, financial analysis is rooted in the real, historical analysis of labor in the capitalist mode of production, its division, breakdown, and recomposition as a technical process. Both mentally and economically, finance is an expression of the tendency for capitalist industry to become ever more centralized and concentrated into fewer hands and locations, to get denser as capitalists pursue efficiency by replacing labor power with the means of production.

Individual businesses pursue higher productivity by rational-izing their operations, adding and upgrading machines in the labor process while deleting humans from it. Reducing costs through the greater efficiency of mechanized techniques makes it possible to gain an advantage over competitors by undercutting them with lower selling prices. As capitalism is a global system of production, the surplus value of these investments flows into a global pool of money capital, the fount of the financial system, overseen by the giant banks and asset management firms who supervise the world's wealth. This growing pool serves as a common source of credit for the capitalist class as a whole, as individual companies borrow from financial institutions to fund their investments, to expand, to acquire other assets, and so on. In turn, manufacturers and commercial companies pay interest on their loans, which is capitalized as staggering amounts of fictitious capital on the balance sheets of the financial firms. The financiers also make money borrowing and lending to each other, of course, which they do constantly. But the true source of financial profits is the interest paid by the other forms of capital; finance produces no value of its own, but only appropriates value that has already been produced elsewhere. Hence, these payments are ultimately deducted from the profits of industry.

To briefly reprise the analysis introduced in Chapter Three: as credit, the flow of money capital greatly facilitates the mechanization and expansion of producers, boosting profits through higher productivity rates. For the first innovators replacing labor power with machines, the benefits are substantial, allowing them to appropriate a larger share of the global surplus value as profits. But the advantage this confers can only be temporary. At the global level, as particular mechanized techniques spread and become the general norm that capitalists everywhere are forced to adopt, the source of surplus value in unpaid labor time dries up, as the part of production performed by exploited laborers decreases relative to the total expenditures of private businesses. The global pool of surplus value available for redistribution as profits shrinks relative to the total invested capital worldwide. Over time, this puts downward pressure on the rate of profit for all productive capitals, forcing them to further revolutionize production, to cut costs even more through technical improvements. The cycle is reset, but this time at a higher base rate of productivity. Consequently, the general result at the level of the productive system as a whole is a permanent condition of overproduction, as mechanization puts downward pressure on the overall rate of profit, which only calls forth additional mechanization as the remedy. The arena of the world market is where the drama plays out, but the competitive battle of the market is only a secondary stage of the deeper pressures caused by the contradictory logic emerging from within production itself. This self-reinforcing dynamic is the core engine of the global economy, a spiraling pattern that is in effect a doom loop built into the heart of capitalism.[31]

Unable to adapt to the new production norm, some businesses go under, or are swallowed by larger companies. Profit is redistributed, temporarily raising the rate of profit for the remaining survivors. Many bankrupt concerns, however, manage to keep operating on credit from banks—including central banks—who often have a stake in keeping obsolete firms alive in order to protect their own interests. The massive federal bailout of 2009, for example, is the only reason the major u.s. automobile companies General Motors and Chrysler—the latter now owned by the global conglomerate Stellantis—still exist today. Some of the biggest manufacturers also pursue their own sources of financial revenue in order to survive, blurring the distinction between "financial" and "non-financial" firms. Apple is a perfect example.

A nominal manufacturing company that owns no factories but has an enormous financial arm six times larger than its "productive" assets, the flagship of American capitalism trades securities, pursues acquisitions, buys back its own stock, and chases other means of financial revenue instead of investing or innovating in its supposed core purpose of production. The more financial dealing displaces production, the more finance itself becomes a powerful engine of deindustrialization. Financial wealth grows as productive capital, the ultimate source of profit, evaporates, a process that obviously has a built-in limit.

These dynamics explain the apparent paradox of astronomical financial profits and declining economic performance. Since the early 1980s rising financial profits have closely tracked stagnating or declining macroeconomic indicators in the United States, such as rates of investment and productivity.[32] As the u.s. economy has been decimated by deindustrialization, labor productivity has slid downward, going from a postwar average growth rate of about 4 percent per year to hovering around 1 percent from the period between 2011 to 2019.[33] In terms of real value added over the same period, which is its total output adjusted for inflation and less the costs of intermediate products used in production, overall rates of growth have declined from an average of 3.7 percent to 1.8 percent.[34] Looking specifically at the manufacturing sector for the more recent period of 1987 to now, labor productivity increased significantly until about 2010, when it leveled off and began to stagnate. Capital productivity, which measures the efficiency of the services provided by capital assets over time, has plummeted a full third since 1987, coinciding with the rise of the vaunted "information age" and putting paid to any lingering hopes for an IT-led productivity revolution.[35] Among other things, abysmal rates of productivity make capital expenditures pointless for businesses, who consequently have little reason to make new investments. Perhaps most significantly, the exhaustion of the capitalist economy shows up as an explosion of corporate debt, a reflection of the dearth of profitable investment and the growing share of financial profits on corporate balance sheets. In 2019 the debt-to-surplus ratio for U.S. non-financial businesses reached 9.5, meaning the debt load for the average American corporation is 9.5 times its profit rate—and this is before the COVID-19 pandemic.[36]

Flatlining productivity and output are the effects of weak business investment; weak investment, in turn, is due to the fact that the rate of profit in the United States is too low for it to make sense for most corporations. As explained in Chapter Three, the profits of U.S. non-financial companies mainly come from monopoly (or monopsony) positions in global value chains, offshore manufacturing, and rents from intangible products like intellectual property, patents, and financial securities. In this global configuration, domestic investment in the United States is not competitive, but financial investing remains so as long as it can siphon part of the profits produced by industrial capital. U.S. stagnation is structural, a built-in feature of the global system as it is currently organized. The great centralization of capital in its financial form over the last four decades, with the USA at its core, is the other side of the massive concentration of capital in its productive form, mainly in Asia: two departments of the same planetary factory. But the factory is breaking down as the source of profits dries up.

The sclerosis of the American economy is a symptom of the broader disease afflicting world capitalism. As the race for ever higher productivity erodes the source of surplus value in unpaid labor time, it generates additional pressure for still higher rates of productivity. Capital confronts its own internal limit in the contradiction that even as capitalists struggle to sever themselves from any connection with human labor, the system as a whole remains dependent on unpaid labor time as the ultimate source of profit. So those lucky enough to still have a job must work even longer and harder merely to sustain an expiring economic system. This is why "labor-saving technologies" further enslave us to work instead of liberating us from it, making some overworked, burnt out, and dissipated, and others unemployed, underemployed, or suicidal. The way this contradiction plays out across the capitalist economy is like the experience of running on an accelerating treadmill: everyone must run faster, always faster, just to remain in the same place.[37]

Diremption

Since the early 1980s, governments the world over have had to borrow and spend ever more to sustain already meager rates of private capital investment. For global financial markets to function "efficiently," governments have been forced to involve themselves ever more intricately in their basic mechanisms. To varying extents this is true of Japan, China, the United Kingdom, and the European Union, all financial powers in their own right, but it is especially true for the United States, whose fate is tied to the international capitalist order made in its image, and whose center it is.

The United States carries out this role through its governmental institutions, above all the Federal Reserve and the Department of the Treasury. In effect, u.s. government debt is the raw material of the global financial system. In a typical bond auction, the Treasury sells debt to primary dealers, a core group of about two dozen investment banks with familiar names, like Citigroup, Bank of America, and J. P. Morgan Chase.[38] These dealers then make the market for u.s. public debt by trading the securities with counterparties throughout the system, who are normally happy to hold the safest assets available for a modest return. In this way, u.s. Treasury bonds function as stabilizers, providing a safe investment when risks are rising. They also usually serve as the most secure collateral for lending, that is, for credit creation. This happens chiefly through repurchase agreements, or "repo." Repo contracts allow holders of safe assets, like u.s. debt, to swap them as collateral for short-term cash; the firm or fund taking the collateral can then, in turn, resell it forward to raise additional cash, fueling further credit creation throughout the financial system. Funds raised in this way are then invested in all types of assets, driving up prices across the system. The Fed uses repo contracts constantly to manage cash balances in the system, as do companies of all kinds to manage their funding and liquidity needs. Global money markets need a steady supply of safe assets to continue functioning at all, and financial profits need a growing supply of such assets to continue growing themselves. Because of its indispensable role as a collateral factory for this distended system of growth, u.s. government debt will continue to rise precipitously, regardless of whatever ideology policymakers and economists are entertaining at a particular time.

To expand the amount of cash in the system, central banks buy government bonds from banks and dealers, removing them from circulation. Since 2008 the Fed has sluiced over $7 trillion of newly created dollars onto private balance sheets in exchange for corporate and government bonds. Since April 2020 alone, the central bank balance sheets of the G10 countries have ballooned over $8 trillion. Through their "large-scale asset purchase" programs—a euphemism for simply shoveling newly printed money at banks and businesses—the central banks must always do more to keep the entire system running by expanding their balance sheets as much as needed, to expand them indefinitely, if need be—"whatever it takes," in the words of the former European Central Bank president Mario Draghi.

Besides the sheer quantity of state intervention, its quality also continues to evolve. Responding to the coronavirus shock in concert with the Treasury, for the first time ever the Fed bought corporate bonds on the private bond market from companies such as Microsoft, Apple, and AT&T. The monetary authorities formed a special purpose vehicle (SPV), basically a legal construct to avoid public oversight of financial transactions, to buy the shares from exchange-traded funds, which are funds whose shares contain bundles of securities that track the overall market. Like repo, SPVS are key to the mechanics of shadow banking discussed in the last chapter. The Fed also committed to buying newly issued bonds directly from corporations, bypassing the usual bank intermediaries, though in the event it did not need to—the public commitment to buy securities endlessly, if needed, was enough to calm the markets.[39]

The footprint of public institutions in the "private" financial system has become so enormous that even central bankers have been forced to acknowledge their expanding role. Rather than the traditional function of acting as a lender of last resort, managing the occasional financial panic in otherwise normal conditions, Andrew Hauser of the Bank of England argues that in the face of normalized market dysfunction, they must embrace their role as market makers of last resort, working constantly to sustain a private sector that can no longer stand on its own feet.[40] The overall trend is clear. The scope for markets as a distributional mechanism is narrowing, their functions gradually rendered redundant as they are displaced by the administrative decisions of government agencies. Through force of necessity, the central banks and treasury departments are gradually euthanizing the market to preserve a social order well past its due date.

The structure of private finance itself has dwindling need for market mechanisms. Consider index funds, passive investment vehicles with a portfolio built automatically to mimic the performance of a particular market index, such as the S&P 500. Since 2008, the share of the equity assets managed by index funds has grown 450 percent, greatly outperforming traditional, actively managed funds and surpassing them in money held in 2019.[41] It is no accident that this rapid rise has coincided exactly with the expansionary policies of the central banks since the Great Financial Crisis. Returns for passive investment depend on the total value of the entire market always going up, which in turn depends on the removal of systemic risk. This is precisely what the expanding administrative reach of the government institutions, particularly the Fed, aims to do.

Operated mainly through just a few giant fund managers who own half the equity assets in America, passive investment makes a joke of the notion of competitive innovation.[42] Not only does it remove any need for acumen while investing money, effectively de-skilling the trade, but it instills incentives to suppress competition between corporations themselves. The asset management firms BlackRock, Vanguard, and State Street Global Advisors are the largest single shareholders in nine out of ten companies on the S&P 500, on average owning more than 20 percent of the shares of every company on the index, so it is naturally in their interest to discourage any competition that could lower profits.[43] This great centralization of ownership in just three companies has led some liberal pundits to complain that index funds are even "worse than Marxism," which is funny since index funds are founded on two seminal ideas of capitalist finance, modern portfolio theory and the efficient markets hypothesis.[44] BlackRock, the largest of the big three, now serves as an essential governing partner to the Federal Reserve and the U.S. Treasury, who commissioned the firm to carry out state purchases of mortgage-backed securities and corporate bonds in the meltdowns of 2008 and 2020, respectively.[45]

The giant asset managers themselves are the result of a decades-long centralization in which the world's firms and households have pooled their collective savings into one gigantic reservoir of financial wealth. Pension funds, insurance companies, corporate profit hoards, university endowments, sovereign wealth funds—massive institutional investors like these are the fount of what Michael Howell terms "global liquidity."[46] Through the repo channels of the financial system, this reservoir serves as the common source of funding for private enterprises and governments alike whose survival no longer depends upon overcoming the competitive challenges of the market, but mainly upon the availability of funds and the willingness of lenders to roll over their outstanding debts for another day.

Finance, as the thickening nexus of government administration with private asset management, increasingly functions as a global administrative system, growing in its scope and power as competitive markets become obsolete. Its evolution into a governmental apparatus has been made possible by centralization in the ownership and control of money, and has been made necessary to ensure that the collective surplus product of a shrinking global workforce continues to be extracted upward into private hands as profit, especially the hands of u.s. banks and businesses.[47] This is not because officials at the Fed and Treasury are lackeys of the big banks—though, of course, they may indeed be that. Rather, it is because they are playing a role it is necessary for them to play: maintaining, in the face of an eroding basis for profits, a life support apparatus for the private, market-based system on which the survival and political legitimacy of the u.s. state itself depends.

Under the pressurizing force of one pulverizing crisis after another, this private–public fusion has evolved to support rising asset prices above all else, because if the credit stops flowing, and the prices stop rising, the game is up. The resulting devaluation of formerly profitable investments would be on a scale scarcely imaginable, wiping out hundreds of trillions in balance sheet assets overnight. Government officials know and fear this, so they go on bailing out bankrupt companies, issuing state debt, and shoveling dollars into the financial system by the trillion. In this growth regime, a general rise in prices is intolerable because it erodes the value of the debt the whole brittle edifice is built upon, so central banks—especially the Fed—fight it tenaciously. Technically all of this can go on as long as security dealers are willing to freely trade u.s. bonds. But socially, the consequences are enormous. All debt is ultimately a claim on future profits that are yet to be produced. As governments are forced to mortgage an ever rising portion of the social product to the needs of the credit system, as total debt rises while total profits fall, there will be ever less social wealth available to provide the basic resources that society needs to materially reproduce itself. Wealth inequality between those who own assets and those who don't, already staggering, will only continue to get worse. The accelerating centralization of wealth, the growth of a surplus population with no place in the economy, the breakdown of politics into competing mass psychoses, spreading domestic turmoil, the general unaffordability of life—eventually, the ever mounting social and political costs of the asset growth economy will reach a breaking point. It is only a matter of time.

As the premier capitalist country, the United States essentially takes on the mounting costs of reproducing the deteriorating conditions for global capitalist production, which show up as an exploding Fed balance sheet and national debt. At the same time, the expansion of governance into private finance and of finance into government erodes the basis for the market's competitive function. The further this dynamic progresses, the more the scope for the market shrinks; the more the market shrinks, the less profitable private production becomes relative to the revenues to be collected through finance; the less profitable private production becomes, the more the accumulation of capital is exhausted, requiring ever more drastic state intervention just to keep its heartbeat going at the present, insufficient levels, which further erodes the basis for the market.

Ironically, the overall effect of these support measures is to lock in the deepening sclerosis of the global economy which makes them necessary in the first place, trapping u.s. society in a spiraling downward pattern of declining labor productivity, political paralysis, and social disintegration.[48] Calls to boost aggregate demand through state-led investment, to "de-financialize" the economy, underestimate how deeply the u.s. state itself is enmeshed in world finance, how its interests are determined by the needs of this system just as much if not more than any domestic concerns. As long as there is no political movement that could force the issue, state actors will not jeopardize these needs. Moreover, with government expenditure pushing 40 percent of GDP, they are not voluntarily going to make that percentage larger than it already is, and in fact will be preoccupied with reducing it to make more room for private profits in a slowing growth environment—that is, for the economic health of the corporate class they ultimately serve. Forced to uphold a global system whose survival depends upon the deterioration of its own domestic economy, the u.s. state is ripped apart from within, its ruling class disorganized and confused, its political class apparently incapable of grasping the source of this crisis, much less acting to address it. The Sisyphean labor of post-neoliberal governance prolongs the lifespan of a world economy in stasis at the cost of condemning the United States to the slow unraveling of a society without a future.

Midnight in America

The eyeless effigy of Ceres shining atop the tower at 121 West Jackson Boulevard in Chicago is thus an apt avatar of finance. Like finance, she seems to see both everything and nothing, the algorithmic, impersonal face of what capitalism has become. Once, she oversaw the advent of the financial knowledge that eventually gave u.s. capitalism a new lease on life at the dawn of the neoliberal era. Perhaps now, at the close of that era, and as was her role in ancient society, she will close the cycle of life and death, an undertaker guiding a dead master to the underworld of past empires.

Still, the Keynesian dream dies hard. If only the elites could get their shit together, if only they would truly decide to act in the public interest, if only our political dysfunctions could be suspended in the name of a common cause, a new era of prosperity and power awaits the United States. But this kind of attitude does not see that the political dysfunction is a direct symptom of the underlying economic disease, of a structural contradiction between the needs of the world economy and the self-reproduction of American society. Observing the fact that the government can apparently spend without limit, neo-Keynesians do not look too far into why it is doing so, mistaking a profound weakness for a sign of strength. So there will be no policy solution to the problems America faces, because no such solution, at least on the national level, exists. But of course, that's what war is for.

Those who wish to avoid such a fate organize themselves on the terrain of the global crisis. National policies cannot undo the secular trend toward economic breakdown because it is bigger than any one nation, its sources transnational. As productivity growth evaporates, corporations will rely even more on wage repression and forcing people to work harder and longer for less. At the same time, embattled national governments, finding themselves without any other expedient, will have to rely more on outright repression instead of growth to deal with a growing mass of humans rendered redundant by an economy that no longer has any use for them. In short, the future is one of intensifying class conflict. Turning it toward class *confrontation* will require fresh concepts for how we think and act in the world together to shape the future into something more like the one we need—that is to say, how we think and act politically.

six

Becoming

"But isn't knowing what is about to happen useful precisely for those who want to stop it happening—for finding the ways, the forms, the forces to make sure it doesn't happen? What other point would it have?"

—MARIO TRONTI[1]

The June air baked like breath exhaled from the sizzling asphalt beneath our feet. There were no cars to be seen on Lake Shore Drive, one of Chicago's busiest thruways. Instead there were only people—at least a few thousand of us in this particular column snaking its way north. From the Loop, the core of the city's sprawling downtown, we had just crossed the Chicago river into Streeterville, an affluent neighborhood on the city's Near North Side where shell-shocked eyes peered down from darkened windows at the streaming mass stretching a mile or more into the southern distance. Police helicopters droned overhead, earning a mass salute of middle fingers and inviting a chorus from below that would become the anthem of the summer of 2020: *"one-two-three-four-five-six-seven-eight-nine-ten-eleven-fuck twelve!"*[2] Riots had erupted in the Loop the night before when a recording went viral showing Derek Chauvin, a white Minneapolis cop, casually executing George Floyd, a Black man who had used a counterfeit bill to buy cigarettes, possibly without knowing it. Ignoring

Floyd's pleas for air and several bystanders begging him to stop, Chauvin used his knee to pin Floyd to the ground by the neck until he suffocated.

Violence was in the air. Colorful placards dotted the top of the crowd, a usual feature of demonstrations like these. But this time felt different. You could cut the tension in the air with a knife. It felt as if every demonstrator was part of one teeming mass of rage. It overflowed—rage toward the homicidal racism of the police; rage toward a homicidal government that requires workers to expose themselves to a deadly new virus in order to maintain "critical infrastructure," a euphemism for maintaining the conditions for corporate profits, all while its protectors of the peace brutally murder its own citizens in the streets; and rage toward the homicidal economic system it serves, a corporate system that sacrifices life for profit, that must subject some workers to the risk of deadly infection because it runs on their labor power, and that consigns the rest to workless misery because businesses can no longer afford them. The class dimensions of the crisis were lost on no one when the banks and businesses were quickly made whole again by $5 trillion in emergency state spending in the early days of the pandemic, while vast numbers of people were simply abandoned, left to waste in newfound joblessness with barely a pittance in state support. You could not ask for a clearer demonstration of how capitalism prioritizes private wealth over human life.

More people joined with every neighborhood we passed through, steadily swelling our ranks, furious eyes searching for an outlet, for some object. The police kept their distance. Anyone who has participated in collective action knows to expect to be outnumbered by police, usually whole columns of the faceless, armed servants of property decked out in military surplus gear. But again, this time was different, because it was the police who were greatly outnumbered. Reports of similar eruptions across the country continued to come in as we marched, now making our way back south to converge with several other crowds. We were heading toward the drawbridges in the heart of the Loop, almost all of which were now raised as if to stall an advancing army. Massing where North Michigan Avenue meets the Chicago River, there was no program, no speech, no plan, only seething agitation, a sense of rising pressure. Different chants started up in different parts of the crowd, swelling louder. A group of people climbed on top of an empty police cruiser to dance; some kids broke its windows with their skateboards, others spray-painted "FUCK 12" across its doors, on the walls of buildings and traffic signs. A phalanx of mounted riot cops approached us from the north, now hesitating for a moment, but their nightsticks readied. Their horses seemed spooked by the sight and sound of the crowd. The chanting grew louder. Some of us exchanged nervous looks. Were the police really going to slice their way through a crowd this thick, this furious? Bottles and trash began to fly. As their captain gave the order to advance, the chants melted into one roaring crescendo, overture to that coming summer scream.

Woe to June!

Cities across America burned in the early summer of 2020. A police station in Minneapolis, epicenter of the uprising, went up in flames. A survey then reported that over 50 percent of the U.S. population thought such measures were justified.[3] Images of charred police cruisers, overturned paddy wagons, and city blocks enveloped in teargas filled 24-hour news networks, while dumbstruck talking heads struggled to narrate what they were seeing. For about two weeks following Memorial Day, the rhythms of everyday life in the city were replaced by the time of urban conflict. Phrases were replaced by deeds. Unafraid to fight the police, enraged crowds faced down squads of riot cops in running street skirmishes, as the overwhelmed forces of order found themselves unable to carry out their basic tasks of suppression and dispersal. Demonstrators in balaclavas advanced on them by forming phalanxes of umbrellas, capable of withstanding a barrage of nightsticks. Protesters in Chicago built makeshift barricades out of dumpsters pulled from alleys into the middle of major downtown streets. Seattle's East Precinct was abandoned by the police after weeks of such street battles, ceding its district to the demonstrators. Property was destroyed, glass broken, stores looted in a frenzy of anti-capitalist violence. The National Guard was deployed in dozens of Democratically run cities. In the nation's capital, Republican president Donald Trump cowered in an underground bunker as crowds besieged the White House, military helicopters circling high above. The multitude, the many, had once again roared to life as a force in history, on a scale and with a ferocity that caught the American ruling class by surprise.

They had cause for concern. Even the sacred order of private property was not respected—a worrying development for the business elite and their state servants, given the fluid situation in the early days of the uprising. In terms of participation, the events of that violent season constituted the largest domestic insurrection in the United States since the 1960s, maybe its largest ever. Early estimates had anywhere from 15 to 25 million people participating in the opening weeks of June.[4] Propelled by the young, these multiracial demonstrations against one of the most extreme forms of entrenched racism, anti-Black state violence, saw people from every ethnic background participating in unprecedented numbers, including many white people.[5] They included the employed and unemployed, those with and without college degrees. And they reached beyond the major metropolitan areas, mobilizing hundreds of thousands in small and mid-sized towns across the country. It was as if a dam had burst.

Predictably, liberals joined hands with fascoids in morally condemning the violence. The apostles of the market will not tolerate desecrations of the temple of property. As soon as talk gives way to action, all the hollow phrases of liberal politicians about racial equality, all the grand myths of the bootlicker right about the unity of the American family, and all the supposedly incommensurable differences between these sworn enemies are quickly forgotten as Democratic mayors heed the reactionary call to crush the rebellion of the underclass. As Marx once said, the party of property, regardless of its political color, only takes one approach when the market order is threatened.[6] When the June uprising cloaked itself in the republican ideals of freedom, equality, and justice for all people, the bickering guardians of the republic responded in one voice: "Woe to June!"

It is thus fitting that the institution representing the repressive arm of the state in the most visceral way, the police, served as both catalyst and object of the movement. In the country with the largest imprisoned population in the world, police brutality against Black people calls forth the masses in a way that no other issue does. From one point of view, the hot summer of 2020 was only the continuation of a long, slow burn. Following the suburban insurrection in response to the police killing of Michael Brown in Ferguson, Missouri, in 2014, similar sequences of struggle unfolded in Baltimore in 2015, then Baton Rouge in 2016, when the deaths of Freddie Gray and Alton Sterling at the hands of the police ignited riotous mobilizations involving thousands of demonstrators lasting for weeks. The pattern is no accident.

The armed guardians of private wealth kill people every day. Since 2013, U.S. police have been responsible for an average of 1,100 deaths per year. As is well documented, this concentrated display of state violence is disproportionately directed at people of color. The year 2021 set a new annual record for police killings, when officers killed 1,136 people, 28 percent of whom were Black, despite Black citizens making up 13 percent of the population.[7] Unarmed Black people are three times as likely as whites to be fatally shot by the cops. Modern urban police forces are trained to deploy as if occupying hostile territory, literally receiving training in counter-terrorism tactics like racial profiling, surveillance, and crowd control.[8]

But the direct application of force is only the tip of a much greater institutional spear: America's uniquely massive system of imprisonment. The land of the free throws more of its population behind bars than any other country on the planet, including China, which has a population four times as large. According to the Prison Policy Initiative, "Not only does the U.S. have the highest incarceration rate in the world; every single U.S. state incarcerates more people per capita than virtually any independent democracy on earth."[9] Until recently, the United States had more of its own people locked up in its prisons than did the USSR at the height of the regime of Joseph Stalin. Again, these measures are visited disproportionately upon Black communities. Black inmates make up almost 40 percent of the nearly 2 million incarcerated Americans, while their rate of incarceration is 2,306 per 100,000 compared to 450 per 100,000 among white people.[10]

Incarceration rates for Black Americans began to rise precipitously in the late 1970s, skyrocketing throughout the next two decades.[11] Uncoincidentally, the explosion of incarceration runs in near-perfect parallel with the acceleration of industrial offshoring, factory closures, automation, and the ensuing evaporation of manufacturing work in urban communities that were often built entirely around it as their main source of employment. In the mid-1980s, official Black unemployment reached 22 percent.[12] Deindustrialization decimated the entire industrial working class, but Black workers bore the brunt of it, as the radical James Boggs predicted they would in his book *The American Revolution*. Boggs stressed how Black laborers were usually the first to lose their jobs in a capitalist economy that can only grow by continually expelling workers from its core, technologically progressive industries.[13] His prediction is borne out in the uneven impact of economic trends like unemployment.

As measured by government agencies like the Bureau of Labor Statistics (BLS), unemployment rates among Black workers are typically twice as high as among whites, rising to three times as high during capitalism's frequent meltdown periods. Likewise for rates of underemployment, a broader measure reflected in what economists call the "labor underutilization rate," which adds the portion of the labor force technically "employed" but in a part-time or precarious capacity, as well as those who are currently jobless but actively searching for work—those "marginally attached to the labor force," in the BLS's terms. In the aftermath of the 2008–9 economic crisis this rate reached a quarter of the Black workforce, taking nearly a decade to fall below 10 percent on the eve of the coronavirus pandemic.[14] None of this includes the vast numbers who have simply given up looking for work altogether, millions of people who cast their shadow on the official statistics in the form of a steadily declining labor force participation rate since the early 2000s.[15]

Marx points out that the forces of production are also the forces producing repression.[16] In capitalist economies, economic growth—of wealth, of jobs, of means of production—happens alongside the simultaneous growth of surplus populations. In this context, the main function of the police is to regulate that part of the population that has no part in its own society, to erect a *cordon sanitaire* between the dispossessed and the beneficiaries of an economic system that runs on dispossession. Internationally, this trend is plainly visible in the wageless millions cloistered in the vast networks of slums that line the world's metropolitan cores, consigned to live on the scraps of the global economy. This population is conservatively estimated to be more than 1 billion people, or 30 percent of the world's urban-dwelling population, though this is almost certainly an underestimation. After the total number of people living in slums declined significantly over roughly the first decade of the new century, the trend began to reverse course in 2014, with the proportion still growing as of 2019.[17] The United Nations estimates that if current trends continue this number could rise to 3 billion people by 2030.

The United States, of course, has its own uniquely pathological way of dealing with this problem. In lieu of a welfare state, policing and mass imprisonment are the de facto policies by which the United States manages its surplus population, the steadily expanding portion of the people consigned to joblessness, underemployment, and deprivation—essentially to economic non-existence. The structural violence of "criminal justice" is exercised at its most focused point where the brutal American history of racial subjugation meets the class purpose of policing: to protect property by controlling the propertyless. Those cut adrift from a livable economic life, together with the underemployed, underpaid, and overworked, make up today's growing reserve army of labor, whose sense that the system has cancelled their future occasionally manifests in seasons of rage that baptize our cities in flames.

The Splendor and Misery of Populism

So it is no accident that the police have become the cause and object of contemporary social struggles. After every police murder of an unarmed civilian, after every cycle of uprising and repression directed at the part of society that has no part in it, the figure of the cop is further politicized as the racist face of the American class war. The George Floyd rebellion showed how the cop can personify the larger system of corporate domination for a huge, diverse, and combative movement. Of course the movement eventually burned out, subverted from without by outright state suppression and from within by the usual cadre of non-profit professionals and Democratic Party hacks, whose function in such moments is to demobilize and defang them by diverting them into the official channels. But while it lasted it was enough to broach the hard question of power, of the concrete play of opposing forces, on a scale rarely seen in the United States. As a ferocious manifestation of the many directed at the armed servants of the few, it vividly exhibited the horizontal dimension of politics: the consolidation of different groups or tendencies from across society into a single formation focused in the same direction. How the variegated forces animating the rebellion could find expression institutionally, the vertical dimension of politics, remains an open question.[18] In both its theory and practice, populism offered one kind of answer.

From Bernie Sanders's defeat to Donald Trump's victory over Hillary Clinton, to Sanders's second defeat to the election of Joe Biden, the roughly five-year period from spring 2015 to spring 2020 spans the rise and fall of the recent "populist" moment in American politics. Both Sanders and Trump positioned themselves as vehicles for a larger movement opposing a mainstream consensus, in place for decades, which held that free markets and global trade, capitalism unbridled, would produce the best outcomes for society at large if they were simply allowed to play out naturally. From the left, Sanders's campaign positioned itself as the electoral vehicle and political successor of the Occupy movement that had kicked off some four years before. Its assumption was that campaigning on a platform of social democratic reforms clothed in the signature Occupy rhetoric pitting the 99 percent against the 1 percent, the people against the billionaires, would ignite a larger mass movement that could form the basis for a new political majority. It held these assumptions in common with similar parties and campaigns across the world, who were attempting to bridge the gap between mass and party with the same populist strategy. Examining their shared fate is instructive.

The activists who occupied the symbolic centers of American cities in the fall of 2011 were the American link in an international chain of uprisings detonated by the Great Recession. Spreading like wildfire to over fifty countries from 2010 to 2013, the global movement of the squares arose against the backdrop of the austerity measures imposed by governments worldwide in the recession's aftermath. Identifying starting points of historical processes is always tricky, but arguably it all began with Thailand's "Red Shirt" demonstrators, who occupied Bangkok in huge numbers and clashed with the country's military repeatedly in the spring of 2010. The Red Shirts were followed in short succession by massive student protests in the United Kingdom, general strikes in France against pension reforms, anti-austerity demonstrations in Greece, the Spanish *Indignados*, and of course, the revolutions that swept almost all the Arab countries in the spring of 2011. Massive and militant student protests in Chile in the same year sparked a general wave of insurrection that soon spread across that entire country. In early 2012, occupations and mass strikes rocked Nigeria, Africa's most populous country, after the government announced the removal of fuel subsidies.[19] Demonstrations around various causes—though often united by the common theme of worsening economic depression— continued across the world in 2012, if on a slightly smaller scale.[20] Then the relative lull in nation-shaking uprisings ended in May 2013 with the Gezi Protests in Turkey, in which some 3.5 million people across the country mobilized in opposition to the neoliberal autocracy of Recep Tayyip Erdoğan. The common thread running through all of these events was a discourse framing them as the immiserated masses against the corrupt oligarchy—or, in the phrase of the era, the 99 percent versus the 1 percent.

The parties and factions emerging from this global tide, like the Corbyn wing of the Labour Party in the UK, Podemos in Spain, Syriza in Greece, La France Insoumise, the People's Democratic Party in Turkey (HDP), and of course the Sanders wing of the Democratic Party, all practiced a self-consciously populist style of politics. Here, I use the word "populist" not in the centrist sense of any tendency irresponsibly opposing the mainstream, but in the technical sense of a discourse that eschews oppositions between workers and capitalists, the left and the right, to pit "the people" against "the elite." In the Greek, Spanish, and French cases, party leaders explicitly adopted the populist theory of politics articulated by the Argentinian political theorist Ernesto Laclau. Laclau's theory is based on the idea that political coalitions are formed in relation to a figure or image that stands in for a much larger array of demands. To take the Turkish case, the figure of Erdoğan became the focal point for anti-corruption concerns, environmental protection groups, opposition to neoliberal policies, supporters of Turkey's secular constitution, police brutality, free speech, and so on. With everyone concentrating on the same figure but for different reasons, the common antagonist—an "empty signifier," to use Laclau's term—enables diverse, sometimes even conflicting interests to see themselves as a unified political force. Representing something different to each group, empty signifiers become the glue, as it were, that holds together the different identities and interests that form contemporary social movements.

So the theory goes, at least. In practice, the populist turn has yielded mixed results, to put it mildly. Europe's populist parties have either wholly conceded to the austerity measures they initially opposed (Syriza), stalled out in their electoral campaigns (Podemos, France Insoumise), or simply failed to get off the ground in the first place, as in the German Left Party's abortive *Aufstehen* campaign. In the UK and the USA, the Corbyn and Sanders campaigns were both soundly defeated in elections, the former by the clownish Brexiteer Boris Johnson, the latter by Joe Biden, the sleepy scion of the old regime. And in Turkey, the HDP has been repressed into insignificance, its main leaders thrown in prison on trumped-up charges as terrorist sympathizers. Italy's two principal populist challengers—the ideologically amorphous 5-Star Movement (M5S), and the far-right Lega Nord—united to support a government led by one of the European Union's arch-technocrats, Mario Draghi, the personification of everything those parties typically vilify. In country after country, the populist wave has crashed on the shoals of transnational financial power, apathetic electorates, and a resurgent center that effectively capitalizes on both.

Latin America is the outlier to this general pattern, where a resurgent "pink tide" carried leftist governments back to power across the region—in some places, like Mexico and Peru, for the first time.[21] With platforms mixing anti-imperialism, the rights of Indigenous peoples, socialized education and healthcare, egalitarian economic development, environmental protection, and a general push for deepening democratic participation, the new left wave in Latin America plays in the populist key of politics. The continent that gave Laclau his classic example of populism, the postwar Argentine regime of Juan Domingo Péron, continues to be one of the world's most politically dynamic regions. Yet these parties and the coalitions that pushed them to electoral victory face daunting terrain. Government debt levels across the region remain high. The world economy remains crippled by the lingering effects of the COVID-19 pandemic, contributing to a new wave of inflation in the Global North. Because a very large amount of the debt owed by Latin American countries is in dollars, they are dangerously vulnerable to rising interest rates in the United States, which could easily trigger a massive recession across the continent, as it did the last time dollar interest rates spiked in the 1980s. And of course, the superpower to the north remains as hostile as ever to any form of democratic or economic self-determination in South America. With this broader context firmly in their minds, the region's well-organized oligarchs and reactionaries are mobilizing to destabilize and undermine newly elected popular governments across the continent.

By abstracting from the language of class and capital in both its theory and its practice, populism opens up the potential for expansive political coalitions of "the people." Yet in the end, this strength is self-defeating. Abstracting from the international geography of class tends to constrict populist appeals to a nationalist frame, because the concept of the people as sovereign entails the modern vehicle of their sovereignty, the nation state. States organized on the basis of nationality presume a notion of collective identity underlying them that cuts across the class divide, both internally and externally: ordinary workers supposedly have more in common with their domestic corporate overlords than with working people in other countries who share their actual conditions of life, whom they are encouraged to see as their competitors. Class collaboration is built into the concept of national sovereignty. In a world divided into independent, competing nation states, appeals to the community of the people only extend as far as the borders that bound it. Competition with other such "peoples" for survival in the capitalist world market is an unavoidable feature of populist politics that cripples its democratic and socialist practitioners.

At the same time, adopting the populist style is a natural advantage for right-wingers, who thrive on this terrain. In particular, it empowers national chauvinists to locate the enemy "elite" externally as a foreign threat to the national community. Then, the enemy without quickly becomes the enemy within, as internal disobedience is demonized as "subversion," "outside agitation," or even "insurgency" somehow connected with the official national adversaries.[22] Dissidence is criminalized for destabilizing the national family. A prominent example from the antisemitic fever swamps of the American right would be the alleged connections between anti-fascist formations (antifa) and the financier George Soros, or when media personalities attempt to paint Black Lives Matter as a PRC-funded organization. Today, the exhaustion of capitalist growth feeds a spreading sense of political paralysis and social crisis that prepares the way for leaders who will supposedly stand up to the evil globalists and their domestic subversives—whoever that may be on a given day.

In some way, authoritarian rule is *always* based on the promise to bring the national family together again in the face of threats from above and below.

Aside from the political liabilities of "the people" as a political frame, populism obscures the actual terrain of power. In practice, populist movements have focused on entering the legislative institutions of representative government in order to expand democratic representation. The assumption is that through steadily building a progressive governing bloc, such institutions could then become the vehicles for realizing a host of long-sought demands around economic, racial, and gender equality. The institutions of liberal democracy may be dominated by wealthy elite interests, the thinking goes, but they themselves are not inherently conservative. Rather, they can be a neutral site of contestation. This is central to the concept of hegemony in populist theory, which it shares with the traditional liberal notion of the neutrality of the state. By articulating the right demands and engaging in ideological clash with elite ideas, popular movements can win broad bases of support, eventually culminating in a new social majority—hegemony—that gives them a democratic mandate to pursue transformative policies. This is the politics of the "national popular," to use the phrase of the classic theorist of hegemony, Antonio Gramsci. But as the experience of the last decade conclusively shows, this misrecognizes the nature of the state.

Capital, Class, and State

Contrary to the theory of hegemony, the state is not neutral. Nor is it simply a steward for the interests of billionaires, directly carrying out their bidding. It is, rather, the specifically capitalist type of state, the nation state, whose impartial, bureaucratic form, based on the division between politics and economics, is an expression of its class nature. The governments of capitalist countries are charged with the task of safeguarding the order of private ownership and market exchange that they presuppose and that ideologically legitimates them. The modern institutions of property and the market, in turn, presuppose an economy founded on the production of commodities, of products and services made explicitly to be exchanged for their owner's enrichment, rather than consumed or used by the actual producers. This implies an opposition between those who control the means of production in order to pursue profits, and those who do the work, but who are separated both from the means of production they use as well as from their own product, which is taken by the owner to be sold. So in practice, safeguarding the rule of property and markets means preserving the class relation between workers and capital, so that capital may continue to appropriate the surplus product of labor power—the condition of expansion for economies organized on a capitalist basis.

In such economies, all commercial and productive activities are undertaken to obtain profit, interest, or rent, the portion of the total social product produced by the working class that is greater than what it needs to reproduce itself. In other words, the goal is to obtain the surplus value created by the class that is greater than what that class needs to reproduce its ability to work, the value of its labor power, which workers receive in the form of wages. So the system runs on exploitation. But this presents a conundrum. As an economic entity, the corporation is concerned with profits, not the well-being of its workforce. Because its primary goal, its raison d'être, is to extract profits, there is a natural pressure to push workers to go ever longer, ever harder, with minimum pay, so that fixed capital will be utilized efficiently, costs minimized, and returns on investment maximized. To the corporation, workers are not people, but investments, subject to the same push for profit maximization as any other invested capital. Taken by itself, if the logic of exploitation were allowed to fully play out, then at some point, pay would fall below the value of labor power, making it difficult if not impossible for the working class, the source of surplus value, to reproduce itself any longer. The logical endpoint of private employment is the destruction of its own employees, the ultimate source of profits. Built-in contradictions like this are why the state must step in as a general authority. Its foremost responsibility is the preservation of capitalist social relations against the tendencies of capital itself. In this kind of society, class domination assumes the form of public administration by necessity.

In the modern era, the nation state is the universal form taken by political rule because it expresses the equally universal and modern concept of popular sovereignty. It serves—at least in theory—to represent the democratic will of its people. Yet the class relations of production are built into the very DNA of the nation state, which expresses them through the politics of the general interest. Since these class relations are transnational, a relationship between the global working class and the equally global capitalist class extending beyond the borders of any one country, the national form of rule is incoherent, because the class domination that is built into it makes true self-government impossible. The distinctly modern ideal of popular sovereignty, of a unique people ruling in its own name and determining its own fate, cannot be realized within the form of the nation state.

To illustrate with a pertinent example: U.S. officials prosecute a new Cold War against China in the name of self-determination. Supposedly the tight links between the United States' and China's economies have become "national security risks," requiring the former to decouple from the latter by relocating more of its industry back home. This, ideally, will power an industrial revival that could restore national prosperity. But the two countries remain dependent on one another in a way that cannot be pried apart so easily: U.S. banks and financial corporations need access to China's enormous financial market to secure their future profits, and China's industrial companies still need access to the lucrative U.S. consumer market for their continued growth.[23] Moreover, as explained in earlier chapters, U.S. domestic businesses need cheap imports to keep the value of workers' wages down, while its multinationals depend on the exploitation of foreign labor, especially in China. Corporations from both countries depend on these arrangements for their continued profitability, arrangements that national governments can try to destroy in the name of the national interest, but only at the cost of destroying the economic basis of their power, and thus their continued existence as political entities.

Thus the notion of national self-determination is inherently irrational. But this contradiction only fuels international competition between nation states, and strengthens national consciousness, precisely because the ideal is impossible to achieve, a vision of harmony forever receding beyond the horizon with every disappointing GDP growth report, every admission that national economic policies are not doing enough to help the people, the inevitable mantra intoning the need to raise global competitiveness, like some broken record stuck on the same line for decades.

Each nation state occupies a different location in the transnational division of labor that organizes the production, transportation, distribution, and consumption of commodities. A country like the United States, for example, features low average labor productivity, a metastasizing financial sector, and the mass consumption of cheap imports largely on the basis of credit. By contrast, countries like China and Germany feature relatively high labor productivity, lower consumption, and a growth regime built mainly around exporting goods to foreign markets. Each country features a different political constitution: the United States is a presidential system with a bicameral legislature; Germany is part of the European tradition of parliamentary, coalition-led government with a chancellor or prime minister figure at its head; and the People's Republic of China still understands itself to be the communist workers' state constructed by Mao-Tse-Tung following the Chinese Revolution. Despite these differences, each country is organized as a nation state whose government claims to represent the will and express the self-determination of its people. Likewise, each of them is structured at their core around a regime of privatized economic life in which workers, the immediate producers, do not own the means of production. Rather than producing for people or purpose, workers' labor in each of these countries produces for profit, for the enrichment of both domestic and foreign owners of the means of production. Each country is part of an international system of nation states competing within the imperialist hierarchy of world capitalism to remake it in their favor. As such, their governments are all subordinated to the need to expand capital by appropriating the surplus product of labor, on pain of extinction. But as the International Labor Organization has reported, the world's workforce has nearly stopped growing.[24] And a shrinking labor pool means a shrinking surplus product of labor.

In a global environment of slowing overall growth, escalating competition over a shrinking surplus drives a fusion of public and private power across all major states, regardless of their particular political constitutions or ideological complexion. As analyzed in the previous chapters, governments are forced to administer the private economy on an increasingly drastic scale merely to sustain current, already insufficient rates of growth. This is the relevant context for understanding the contemporary political terrain. Hegemony, the dominance of a particular set of ideas about society, is not won through savvy discursive articulation, which would then—as populist theory has it—open up the space for radical political or economic change. Rather, radical change happens in the form of economic crisis, leaving policymakers and ideologists scrambling to conceptualize it after it has already occurred. The ideological hegemony of nationalist discourse today is rooted in the inability of the private capitalist economy to overcome the barriers to its own growth, and the resulting imperative for national governments to reassert state power in an attempt to resuscitate it.

As the last decade and a half has painfully demonstrated, elite policy regimes do not come together on the basis of a rational consideration of ideas, which are then applied through policies. Rather, state actors articulate policies in a more or less haphazard way through pragmatic experimentation in response to constantly shifting circumstances, with theory and ideology evolving to reflect these developments after the fact. Laws, norms, and established precedents count for little when the state's overriding prerogative is not actually to understand economic events, much less to act to shape them, but merely to continue to exist, which in capitalist society means preserving at all costs the existence of a system of market-based private ownership that grows more sclerotic by the day.

In such conditions, the political center will regard the prospect of left parliamentary blocs not as potential governance partners, but as a liability endangering a precarious economic regime in which growth is already scarce, and potentially obstructing the project of international imperial competition over resources and markets. Centrist blocs will therefore adopt the same kind of hostile footing that they would toward any threat to the national interest, which, as already explained, expresses the class relations of domination as they are configured within a particular country. Having responded to the initial shock of 2015–16, when it was caught unprepared by an international upsurge of challenges from both the political left and the right, the center has now adopted an actively combative stance, particularly toward its left flank.

In the name of a dying world, centrist retrenchment has defeated the brief resurgence of social democracy in the Global North. The international parliamentary left in the broad sense has been neutralized, its goals unrealized. States are evolving into a centralized form of neo-imperialist nationalism. War is in the air. Theoretically hobbled and practically exhausted, left-populism has run its course. Yet populist theory still grasps something essential about the conditions of contemporary mass politics. Politics in the current moment does indeed revolve around identities and leader figures, for good or ill; it lives through the viral imagery and communicative ecosystems of the Internet; and it invokes demands—demands for meaningful work, for control over our own time, for a habitable planet, for a life worth living. It involves any collective attempt to imagine and build a new form of life together. Populism's mistake was to believe all this relativized class as just another source of personal identity tied to one's income bracket, and the war against capital as one particular floating signifier among others. In fact, these are but ways of living the class relationship.

Class is not a static economic position one occupies, as in "working class" or "middle class," but one's relative location in the process of production within the global circuit of capital. By performing their different kinds of work, an assembly line worker in Shenzen, a software programmer in San Jose, an indebted graduate student bouncing around the adjunct circuit in Toronto, a retail clerk in Barcelona, a cobalt miner in southern Congo, and a logistics engineer in Mexico City all facilitate the production and distribution of surplus value to the owners of capital, of society's means of materially reproducing itself. In so doing, they reproduce the class basis of the capitalist system, whatever they may imagine about what they do. The class relation and the labor power that reproduces it are a *social and political process*. And as an objective process, they can be subjectively experienced, imagined, and articulated in radically different ways. Class identity is composed on the basis of experience, the experience of those who go without, the dispossessed, the debt-enserfed, the toilers, the mind-broken climbers who finally realize that, no matter how hard they try, they will never be able to get off the hamster wheel. It is not given in advance, but exists only *in potentia*, in the universal experience of alienation from corporate society shared in some way by most of its inhabitants, and rooted in the alienation of labor power from itself, the basic separation on which capitalism is founded.

An expansive definition of class calls for a tactical approach to class politics. I want to offer one such approach in what I will call the three-fold, overlapping perspectives of the Stage, the Shop, and the Street. The boundaries between these three scenes are fluid and permeable. They roughly correspond to a much older conception, originally found in Aristotle, in which politics can be understood in the changing relationships between the One, the Few, and the Many. But the common thread running through each is the concept of mediation: the continuing need for some figure, some vivid image or idea to serve as the focal point for the different lines of force coursing through the masses, serving not as a program or ideology, but as a waypoint, a north star for the scattered fragments of refusal to converge on a common point. That point remains undefined; its content cannot be specified in advance, but it can be dreamed, depicted, screamed. As a political force, class is the unending, myriad actualization of this potential.

The Stage, or the Politics of the Image

Class composition does not happen automatically. It is a staccato process unfolding across the uneven terrain of political and economic conflict. Certain images appear that galvanize the masses. Or a seemingly random incident occurs that draws them forth in their thousands. Something happens that triggers disgust, followed swiftly by outrage. Pictures appall, rumors spread, rage rekindles. The streets forge seething emotions into the bonds of collective action. As people see others begin to act, privately felt emotions undergo catalysis to become shared motives. Seeing others act feeds the desire to act oneself. Outbreaks of class struggle tend to have a viral, explosive character. They unfold with their own internal momentum propelled by the logic of mimesis, by the urge to imitate what one sees.

Politics is inescapably visual. It is mediated by pictures flowing by on screens, by the electoral game, by the talking heads frantically trying to shore up its fading legitimacy, by viral media, by the affirmation of one's own emotions in the sight of others acting. Political images can sharpen the class divide, clarifying it, as when a historically multiracial multitude emerges in response to a graphic recording of racist police brutality, as in the George Floyd Rebellion. And they can do so on an international scale: Floyd's image spread to murals and movements in dozens of countries worldwide in the summer of 2020. They can also blunt its edges, as when politicians or media figures, gesturing toward the cause, solemnly enjoin those same demonstrators to vent their anger at the official outlet, the polls. Media and political institutions both mobilize and demobilize, galvanize and diffuse. They are the Stage, a domain of conflict over the significance and meaning of images.

If class identity is not pre-determined but indelibly shaped by shared experience, then radicals cannot ignore the need to articulate that experience, to depict it as the collective learning process of a class fitfully forming itself. If the symbolic terrain of politics is abandoned by the left, then it will simply be monopolized by the death cults of the right. In an era of rising militarism and xenophobia fueled by escalating Great Power imperialism, itself aggravated by a world economy in decline, this is a serious liability. Populist theory understands this. Its attention to the critical role of mediation for politics remains its most important contribution.

As the theory has it, a unified movement composed of separate tendencies, interests, and goals comes together through floating signifiers in which all the different participants can recognize themselves, or their common enemies. In other words, a horizontal formation of people is given coherence by a vertical figure with which its members can identify. Individual politicians frequently play this role by becoming avatars for a larger constituency. To recall Aristotle's terms, this is the politics of the One. Yet the inherent risk of this kind of politics is an overinvestment in the leader figure, in the vertical dimension of politics. This misplaced verticalism was central to the defeat of the Sanders campaign, which assumed that rising to the highest level of the country's media and political institutions in a presidential election, articulating the right message, and winning the early primary contests would unlock the full power of the disenchanted masses. Yet despite doing these things, the movement did not materialize. A serious power imbalance remained between the insurgent bloc within the Democratic Party and its established regime which, once regrouped, proved easily capable of defeating its upstart adversary. Now, with the center retrenched, the only logical option is to focus on the power imbalance itself.

The Shop, or Work and Its Afterlives

Succinctly, the Shop is the realm of labor in all of its dimensions. It encompasses all conflicts around the direct employment of labor power to extract profits for corporate expansion, the exploitation of surplus labor time through waged or salaried arrangements. Spatially, it includes all workers producing in some way for the world market; temporally, it includes entire lifespans of regimes of economic growth, as these interconnect workers through the global division of labor. Its conflicts follow the faultlines of the global economy, which erupt into earthquakes over crisis cycles that can last for years or even decades. As the concentration of capital makes human labor superfluous even as it continues to depend on it, the Shop is the terrain of the Few, the potential power of workers' organization to impact the critical pressure points of a decrepit capitalist economy.

In the world shop, workers' resistance at the core of the global productive system connects to conflicts at the point where their commodities are turned into money, where the surplus value created by their labor power is realized, because both are part of the same circuit of capital. Despite working for different companies, assembly line laborers in Guangzhou striking over withheld wages and workers in New York organizing the warehouses where the Chinese-made goods wait to be sold occupy two different points in a single global circuit of capital, the production of surplus value and its realization as money. Whatever form they take, conflicts and confrontations organized along these lines are inherently interconnected within the world shop, the immediate process of production.

Consider the evolution of China's Pearl River Delta, erstwhile workshop of the world. In 2011, the PRC government launched a much-vaunted new social insurance law intended to provide, for the first time, a comprehensive social safety net for Chinese workers, including retirement pensions, unemployment insurance, maternity leave, and compensation for workplace injuries. The law came after a major upsurge of labor unrest in the Delta, the industrial heartland of China's rapid growth period. As the world economy cratered in the wake of the Great Recession, a historic strike wave swept across the region, particularly among migrant workers who staffed the region's auto and textile manufacturing centers in Guangdong. Sparked by the outrage at a rash of well-publicized worker suicides at Foxconn-owned factories, the insurgency spread like wildfire to hundreds of factories and involved tens of thousands of workers—70,000 according to Chinese newspapers, likely a significant undercount. Foxconn was and remains one of Apple's principal manufacturing contractors, so production conflicts in the Delta have global ramifications. Work actions in the region continued by the thousands, sporadically but consistently over the next two years, in a country where every strike is a wildcat strike—there are no legal strikes in China.[25] Then, in the summer of 2014, one of the largest walkouts of the decade erupted at a shoe factory in Dongguan, when an injured worker, Cui Tiangang, found out that his employer would not pay him according to the supposedly binding social insurance law. His case was like a match to tinder, igniting a sea of discontent flowing just beneath the surface. Worker outrage erupted into one of the greatest strikes of the decade, involving more than 40,000 workers over two weeks.

It should come as no surprise that since that period of sustained labor militancy, the Pearl River Delta has seen extensive factory closures, as Chinese manufacturing relocates into the country's cheaper, less militant interior.[26] Replaying the familiar pattern that has played out in country after country in the Global North, the industrial base has shed human labor, reorganizing—often as part of official government planning— into a sleeker, more service-based economy with pockets of highly automated manufacturing producing hi-tech goods such as telecommunications, biotechnology, and pharmaceuticals.[27] As its own regional cycles of deindustrialization set in, China's economy is gradually mirroring the world's old industrial core. As a zone of engagement, what I call the Shop includes the forms of workers' activity that directly impact the worldwide capital-labor relation from within, destabilizing it, forcing it to evolve along its spiraling, crisis-ridden historical path. Conflicts over the labor process in the Global South, where most of the world's manufacturing workforce is located, are at the core of this dynamic.

In the expanded sense I am outlining here, the Shop also includes all the supporting work that makes such productive labor power possible—the labor of social reproduction. Reproductive labor sustains the social bonds that underpin any community. Consider education. Teachers play a vital role in both the general formation of the workforce, providing a developmental experience essential for later participation in the economy, as well as its daily reproduction, providing childcare seven hours a day for a society in which both parents must work. Teaching is part of the care economy, the huge portion of social labor dedicated to the needs of children, family members, friends, the old, and the sick. It is also a highly gendered profession, with women making up between 65 and 70 percent of all teachers, the disproportion decreasing as one moves from pre-primary school (97 percent) to college (43 percent).[28] Coded as feminine and including both paid as well as unpaid work, the care sector crosses the boundary between public and private, workplace and household, the needs of markets and of human beings. Again, teaching is a pertinent example, as educational labor is shared between teachers and parents. Healthcare is another, divided between an enormous, commodified, monetized sector and the vast pool of unpaid labor provided by domestic caregivers. Education and healthcare workers occupy strategically critical sectors of the economy because their labor goes toward the formation of labor-power and its reproduction as a vital force.

The years leading up to the pandemic in the United States were some of the most militant since the 1980s, with 2018 seeing nearly half a million workers involved in strike actions; 2019 saw well over 400,000.[29] Teachers were the tip of the spear, leading the largest walkouts of these years totaling hundreds of thousands across a swathe of traditionally conservative states, like Arizona, Oklahoma, West Virginia, and the Carolinas. Post-2020, the brutal working conditions arising from the pandemic, along with a bumbling, brief expansion of the social safety net in response by the u.s. government, emboldened u.s. workers to quit at record rates in 2021 as the economy came back online following the shutdowns of the previous year. Understandably given these conditions, the healthcare sector in particular saw drastic numbers of workers leaving their jobs, as well as a number of high-profile strikes by health workers in hospital systems on the West Coast, Chicago, and Buffalo, New York. Unfolding across the embattled terrain of schools and hospitals, work actions in education and healthcare impact the very capacity of the workforce to reproduce itself—and thus to reproduce the basic requirements for capitalist growth.

Lastly, in addition to production and reproduction, the Shop includes the vast but less visible world of workless life. This is the world of those without regular, waged employment who dwell in zones of abandonment left behind not only by capital, but by entire societies. The deindustrialized wastes of Northern cities, the sprawling slums on the outskirts of megacities in the Global South, the collapsing ecosystems of the American countryside, the far hinterland, where forgotten millions live in places that society has completely written off—surplus populations of humanity made redundant by the contemporary economy, which has no place or use for them.

This population is not a vast labor pool in waiting that could potentially be incorporated into modern economic life, but is rather a constantly reproduced, structural condition of capitalist expansion. As corporations compete for profits by mechanizing the labor process, ever fewer labor inputs are needed to produce the same amount of output. While absolute demand for human labor can still increase with the spread of capitalist production to new areas with fresh populations to exploit, the overall demand for labor relative to output decreases as its overall productivity increases with the progression of the technological frontier of production. If output itself does not increase, or continues to slow down, the result is chronic under- and unemployment on an expanding scale.

The growing reserve army of labor, to use Marx's expression, is both a condition of and a barrier to capitalist growth. Despite their exclusion from formal work arrangements, this population plays a key role in the reproduction of capital, insofar as corporations depend on a surplus reservoir of the under- and unemployed to discipline the labor force. A permanent surplus population keeps downward pressure on wages by discouraging workers to fight for better conditions or even simply to quit, reminding them of the wageless misery that awaits them should they stop working. Likewise, governments criminalize the survival strategies of the workless, sowing divisions between the employed and the unemployed. At the same time, the surplus population poses an immense practical problem for corporate society. Its growth endangers the very foundations of private property and the rule of law. Ferocious social explosions like the George Floyd Rebellion, or the swarming invasions of French cities by the yellow vests (*gilets jaunes*), periodically erupt to remind our corporate overlords of the risks in the game they are playing. These can grow to the level of an existential threat, as happened in the transcontinental uprisings that overthrew regimes across the Middle East and North Africa in 2011–12. In these circumstances, expanded policing and mass incarceration emerge as key state strategies to ensure social reproduction by repressing this population. At the same time, the more obvious it becomes that this is the real purpose of law enforcement, the more openly brutal its tactics, the more illegitimate and widely hated its representatives become. Thus the surplus population is both savior and destroyer of the corporatocracy, a spectral figure haunting the addled minds of its guardians. So do the conflicts of the Shop overflow into those of the Street.

The Street, or the Economy of Violence

The Street is the realm of the multitude, or the Many. Whereas the Shop is the scene of conflicts around the exploitation and reproduction of labor for profit, the growing masses of the Street are the social relations of the capitalist economy disintegrating in real time. They are not responding to its disintegration; they *are* its disintegration, dissolution in human form. The simultaneous necessity and impossibility of a rising surplus of humans, a core contradiction of the capitalist economy, expresses itself in the crisis of an increasingly ungovernable society. Its battlegrounds tend to be the gleaming downtowns or central squares of major cities, sites of running skirmishes between armies of enraged civilians and phalanxes of armored riot police.

The negative character of the multitude is reflected in its distinctly horizontal, anarchic structure. Mass demonstrations, occupations of the public square, are typically leaderless, with defunct ideologies of bygone eras flowing through them from across the political spectrum, from anarchism, to Trotskyism, to twentieth-century trade unionism, to liberal multiculturalism, to democratic self-determination, to xenophobic ethnonationalism, to antisemitism—or all of these at once. Ghosts from the past return to speak through the multitude. Multitudes are internally contradictory, inherently messy assemblages whose incoherence is their main strength. Anyone, for any reason, can join the multitude once it has emerged, once again, onto the Street.

Or it may have little to do with ideas at all. As the injuries and insults stack up ever higher, when the thousand little humiliations of daily life accumulate to a boiling point, when the tension becomes unbearable, the kettle boils over. The result is the reactive, blind fury of the mass riot. Riots are the masses in combat stance. They are akin to a discharge of pure kinetic energy, with no clear object except a burning desire for violence. A widely felt but diffuse sense of outrage can be channeled into action by a particular government policy, such as the removal of subsidies from a key sector like transportation, as in Brazil in 2013, or withdrawing funding from public universities, as in the student demonstrations that rocked Chile beginning in 2011 and eventually culminating in the overthrow of the neoliberal constitution that had ruled the country since the regime of Augusto Pinochet. Or the catalyst can be the viral spread of an image. The self-immolation of the Tunisian street vendor Mohamed Bouazizi in late 2010, or video footage of a cop casually murdering an unarmed civilian, as in the summer of 2020 in the United States. Or as in China, when, in parallel with the wave of revolutionary energy then sweeping the Arab world, the great strikes in the Pearl River Delta during the summer of 2010 were followed a year later with a spectacular, even greater mass insurrection by Sichuan migrant workers in Guangzhou. In an already volatile summer, a twenty-year-old pregnant woman was abused by local police, igniting a firestorm of riots that rampaged through the city for three days. Whether or not it was true did not matter, for the incident became symbolic, representing the oppression of all migrant workers. Everyday routines, the rhythms of daily life, are suspended in such outbreaks of mass violence. In the dilated time of the Street, the crushing pressures of life in capitalist society are shunted aside, its veil of legitimacy torn asunder as the masses in their thousands confront the real conditions of their existence.

Public images like these condense the experience of corporate domination and the brutal regime of normalized violence it rests upon. Personifying it, they allow the public to *see* what this regime does to people, how it literally runs on death, channeling mood into motion like a surge of voltage through conductive metal. In the riot, the multitude retaliates against the deadly coercion of the corporate order and its state apparatus, seeking revenge for past suffering. This in turn invites further crackdowns, as the state is forced to nakedly reveal its real purpose in preserving the property and wealth of that order. At the same time, every act of repression is seared indelibly in the memory of the repressed, sowing seeds of hatred toward the system. The process of the emergence and suppression of the mass riot is the very ground on which it will be summoned forth in even greater size and ferocity in the future. Injury, reprisal, counter-reprisal: the economy of violence shapes the terrain of contemporary politics, forcing governments and oppositions alike to adapt to its rhythms.

Whatever event sets it off, when the multitude assumes combat footing it poses the issue of power in a sharply focused way—the massing of forces at a single point, as in classic, Napoleonic military strategy. Urban police forces can frequently find themselves overwhelmed by the sheer number of citizens they are charged to repress, temporarily losing control, ceding territory. At the same time, the tactics of the multitude evolve, gradually dispensing with the sit-in spirit of the Occupy movement in favor of a more openly confrontational posture. Scrums with police, property destruction, looting, blockades of major urban arteries—motivated by an ever clearer sense that there is no future, the tactical repertoire of the multitude gradually expands, its methods radicalize. Any specific demands are drowned out by the sheer ferocity of pitched battles with the agents of state violence.

These clashes can grow to such an immense scale because they draw forth incursions from—and sometimes take place within—the sprawling suburbs and exurbs ringing metropolitan areas. This industrial fringe on the outskirts of great cities, the "near-hinterland" as theorized by Phil A. Neel, is a critical zone of contemporary production, hosting much of the labor in transportation, logistics, and manufacturing that the global economy depends on.[30] Here, those pushed out from an increasingly unaffordable urban core meet migrants streaming in from the countryside and abroad in search of work, forming immense pools of cheap labor just out of sight of the media-saturated, consumption-driven, college-educated culture of the cities themselves. In the USA, a spatial and cultural barrier divides those who work in these critical sectors from the more educated, higher-paying jobs in finance, communications, digital technology, law, and other business services that cluster in the revitalized downtowns and trendy neighborhoods of the urban centers. This stratified pattern of urbanization in the United States increasingly resembles that of megacities of the formerly colonized world, like São Paolo, Lagos, and Bangkok, where surplus populations struggle to scrape by in the vast, industry-adjacent slums that surround them, and where the distinction between waged employment and daily survival through informal work is often blurred. In the war of the multitude, social conflict is waged across the entire geography of the city and its hinterland, circulation and production.

Composing a Future

Three scenes of revolutionary possibility: the Stage, the Shop, and the Street do not directly map onto physical or institutional spaces. Rather, they are overlapping vectors in an open-ended process of class formation. Emerging on a historical terrain of neo-nationalism born of economic entropy, they represent three fronts in a new class war. This war will be prosecuted from corporate boardrooms and government bureaus as the custodians of capital, in their desperate attempts to remain competitive, struggle to maintain a compliant workforce. It will also be prosecuted from below, as the economic forces pushing toward destabilization virtually guarantee more insurrections to come. The only question is: what form will these take?

Every nation in the capitalist game needs a compliant domestic working class, as well as a quiescent reserve army of labor, to succeed in the game. At the same time, ever more social resources have to be withheld from the general population so they can be channeled into corporate bank accounts in the form of subsidies, tax breaks, tariffs, lucrative government contracts—the whole trough of corporate welfare. Corporate welfare is not a way for government bureaucrats to enrich themselves by giving money away to favored businesses—it is not "crony capitalism." It is rather a necessity for a country's corporations to stay afloat as they lose competitiveness, and a key state strategy for governments attempting to improve or maintain their rank in the global hierarchy. The need to support a private economy that grows more anemic by the day is an unconditional imperative for the stewards of corporate domination, because it is the foundation of that domination. But in this condition of decay, there is only so much to go around. As long as a new dynamic of general growth is not introduced—and I have spent much of this book showing why that is unlikely—private largesse means public deprivation. Profits will continue to come at the expense of real wage growth for the working class and the crumbling remains of the welfare state. Even the regime of wealth creation through the growth of financial asset prices, the asset economy, is on borrowed time. It can only go as long as governments can maintain the default policy regime of asset growth at all costs— a regime that gets harder to sustain as those costs manifest themselves in the mounting social turmoil of a terminal society.

This is the terrain on which the world working class moves. There is nothing pre-determined in the work of class composition. Its potential only becomes actual by confronting the tensions between different sections of the working class, between those with and without work, and between workers across the borders that artificially divide us. The exact shape of what is coming cannot be known in advance, and so neither can its name, if it is to have one. Regardless, everything hinges on the question of class consciousness, a question that extends beyond national boundaries to include those elsewhere with whom we share the idea of freedom.

In the meantime, the river of history flows on, its current quickening and slowing on a timescale of generations. Moments of opportunity open up only to slam shut again. Periods of possibility are succeeded by periods of powerlessness, when the space for action closes and nothing much seems possible anymore. Demobilization sets in. The forces of reaction regroup and consolidate, seemingly even stronger than before. During these doldrums, they congratulate themselves on their managerial genius and far-sighted responsibility, which lasts until the next great crisis outs them as the gormless hacks they are, setting things in motion again. Even when its surface looks calm, the great river does not stop moving. It does not cease but constantly churns beneath the surface, "seething in its depths," as Leo Tolstoy put it.[31] It is only a matter of time before the current picks up once again, sweeping everyone and everything along with it. We cannot know exactly what the future will bring, but what is certain is the status quo is not long for this earth. In fact, it is already passing away at this very moment, like a city built upon a floodplain, engulfed by the rising torrent.

References

Introduction

1 All this is according to Gendron's "manifesto," posted online before the shooting.
2 Shweta Sharma, "Tucker Carlson repeats Racist 'Great Replacement' Theory and Says Democrats Trying to 'Replace the Electorate'," *The Independent*, www.independent.co.uk, July 20, 2022. Carlson has since left Fox News to start a new show on Twitter, now known as "X." The platform was renamed by its brilliant owner, Elon Musk, who was legally compelled to buy it after attempting to back out of his own takeover attempt.
3 "Touch Your Nose if JFK Jr. Is Alive," *Our Great Awakening*, www.ourgreatawakening.org, accessed May 6, 2022.
4 Emma Zafari, "How Social Media Enables Violence and Breeds Conspiracy Theories like QAnon," *Foreign Policy Youth Collaborative*, https://fpyouthcollab.org, January 30, 2021.
5 Ivan Wecke, "Conspiracy Theories Aside, There Is Something Fishy About the Great Reset," *Open Democracy*, www.opendemocracy.net, August 16, 2021.

1 Globalization and Its Double

1 Thomas Friedman, "A Manifesto for a Fast World," *New York Times*, March 3, 1999, section 6, p. 40.
2 Donald Trump, Twitter, https://twitter.com, December 9, 2014.
3 Thomas Friedman, *The Lexus and the Olive Tree: Understanding Globalization* (New York, 1999), p. 102.
4 Andrew L. Shapiro, *The Control Revolution: How the Internet Is Putting Individuals in Charge and Changing the World We Know* (New York, 1999).
5 See Michael Schudson, *The Good Citizen: A History of American Civic Life* (Cambridge, 1998); and Manuel Castells, *Rise of the Network Society* (Hoboken, NJ, 1996), pp. 507–9. Habermas's output is prodigious, but to get a sense of what deliberative democracy was

supposed to be, see his *Between Facts and Norms: Contributions to a Discourse Theory of Law and Democracy*, trans. William Rehg (Cambridge, 1996).

6 Rob Picheta, "The Flat-Earth Conspiracy Is Spreading Around the Globe. Does It Hide a Darker Core?," CNN, www.cnn.com, November 18, 2019; "America's Flat-Earth Movement Appears to Be Growing," *The Economist*, www.economist.com, November 28, 2017; Stephanie Pappas, "Are Flat-Earthers Being Serious?," *Live Science*, www.livescience.com, October 17, 2022.

7 Sigmund Freud, *The Uncanny*, trans. David McLintock (New York, 2003), p. 142.

8 Consider this divination from one of Friedman's classic columns: "We Americans are the apostles of the Fast World, the prophets of the free market and the high priests of high tech. We want 'enlargement' of both our values and our Pizza Huts. We want the world to follow our lead and become democratic and capitalistic, with a Web site in every pot, a Pepsi on every lip, Microsoft Windows in every computer and with everyone, everywhere, pumping their own gas." Friedman, "Manifesto."

9 Politicians, pundits, and philosophers all chanted the new creed in unison. The heroic self-regard among politicians of the time is perfectly encapsulated in former UK prime minister Tony Blair's 1999 "Third Way" speech: "Tony Blair's Full Speech," *The Guardian*, www.theguardian.com, September 28, 1999. Anthony Giddens, sociologist and house intellectual of New Labour, provided the theoretical rationale for the Labour Party's obeisance to capital in *The Third Way: The Renewal of Social Democracy* (Cambridge, 1998). Much of academic philosophy throughout this period was concerned with renovating liberalism as the guiding philosophy for a world that no longer has any alternative to it. Major touchstones include Francis Fukuyama, *The End of History and the Last Man* (New York, 1992); Jürgen Habermas, *The Postnational Constellation: Political Essays*, trans. Max Pensky (Cambridge, 2001); and John Rawls, *Political Liberalism* (New York, 2005).

10 See Dani Rodrik, "Put Globalization to Work for Democracies," *New York Times*, www.nytimes.com, September 17, 2016; Martin Wolf, "Capitalism and Democracy: The Strain Is Showing," *Financial Times*, www.ft.com, August 30, 2016; Lawrence Summers, "How to Embrace Nationalism Responsibly," *Washington Post*, www.washingtonpost.com, July 10, 2016.

11 See for example Yascha Mounk, "How Liberals Can Reclaim Nationalism," *New York Times*, www.nytimes.com, March 3, 2018; and John B. Judis, "What the Left Misses About Nationalism," *New York Times*, www.nytimes.com, October 15, 2018.

12 Robert Kuttner, "Economic Nationalism Becomes Mainstream—and Sensible," *American Prospect*, https://prospect.org, June 15, 2021;

J. W. Mason, "A Cautious Case for Economic Nationalism," *Dissent*, www.dissentmagazine.org, Spring 2017.

13 Gadi Taub, "Steve Bannon Tells *Haaretz* Why the Russians Aren't the Bad Guys and Why He Can't Be an Anti-Semite," *Haaretz*, www.haaretz.com, July 30, 2018.

14 On the proposal for a social index fund, see Matt Bruenig, "A Simple Fix for Our Massive Inequality Problem," *New York Times*, www.nytimes.com, November 30, 2017.

15 As in Judis, "What the Left Misses," and Angela Nagle, "The Left Case against Open Borders," *American Affairs*, https:// americanaffairsjournal.org, November 20, 2018.

16 "The World Is Faster, Deeper, More Fused, Open and Fragile: A Dialogue between Thomas L. Friedman and Wang Huiyao," *China-U.S. Focus*, www.chinausfocus.com, April 20, 2021.

17 Karl Marx, *The Political Writings* (New York, 2019), p. 64.

18 Sebastian Conrad, *What Is Global History?* (Princeton, NJ, 2016), pp. 93–4.

19 Paolo Giussani, "Empirical Evidence for Trends Toward Globalization: The Discovery of Hot Air," *International Journal of Political Economy*, XXVI/3 (Fall 1996), p. 19. The data on U.S. GDP is taken from Angus Maddison, *Contours of the World Economy, 1–2030 AD* (Oxford, 2007), p. 345.

20 A good introduction to the subject from a global point of view is Eric Helleiner, *The Neomercantilists: A Global Intellectual History* (Ithaca, NY, 2021).

21 The idea of a community sharing some intrinsically unique identity is built into the modern word "nation" common in Western European languages: it is derived from the Latin *natio*, roughly meaning birth, breed, or origin, but also used to refer to specific tribes or races of people, a common kinship. Tropes of birth frequently appear in national origin stories as the historical moment at which "the people" were born as a collective body through a founding act, as in the opening of the U.S. Constitution: "We the people . . . ". But *natio* is also the source of the words "nature" and "natural," suggesting an organic phenomenon with a life process of its own, independent from human affairs. This fundamental tension between two senses of time, the time of political creation at a particular moment in history and the timeless qualities of an everlasting nature, is the irresolvable ambiguity at the heart of the national myth. It shows up historically in the always permeable boundaries between civic forms of nationalism, based on citizenship within a politically defined community, and ethnonationalism, the identification of citizenship with one's (unchosen) ethnic or racial background, which then determines one's political destiny. The scholarly literature on nationalism is enormous, but to make an initial cut, one could

do worse than take an overview from three classic texts on the subject: Ernest Gellner, *Nations and Nationalism* (Ithaca, NY, 1983); Eric Hobsbawm, *Nations and Nationalism since 1780: Programme, Myth, Reality* (Cambridge, 1990); and Benedict Anderson, *Imagined Communities: Reflections on the Origin and Spread of Nationalism* (New York, 1983).

22 Friedrich List, *The National System of Political Economy*, ch. 15, www.econlib.org, accessed November 12, 2023.

23 The line appears in the preface to G.W.F. Hegel, *Elements of the Philosophy of Right*, ed. Allen W. Wood, trans. H. B. Nisbet (Cambridge, 1991), p. 23.

24 Conrad, *What Is Global History?*, p. 67.

25 The "long nineteenth century" periodization was proposed by Eric Hobsbawm, who covers the period in the first three books of his monumental history of the modern world: *The Age of Revolution: Europe, 1789–1848* (New York, 1962), *The Age of Capital, 1848–1875* (New York, 1975), and *The Age of Empire, 1875–1914* (New York, 1987).

26 Karl Marx, "Postface to the Second Edition," *Capital: A Critique of Political Economy*, vol. I, trans. Ben Fowkes (New York, 1990), p. 103.

2 Undertow

1 Antonio Gramsci, *Selections from the Prison Notebooks*, trans. Geoffrey Nowell-Smith and Quentin Hoare (New York, 1971), p. 178.

2 Since 2015, the United Kingdom has experienced the lowest GDP growth and fastest inflation in Western Europe. Martin Wolf, "Boris Johnson Must Embrace the Brexit He Made," *Financial Times*, www.ft.com, May 17, 2022.

3 Tom Metcalf, "Richest in Britain Got €25bn Richer Since the Brexit Vote," *Irish Examiner*, www.irishexaminer.com, May 11, 2019.

4 Eleanor Halls, "Emmanuel Macron says France needs a King," GQ, www.gq-magazine.co.uk, May 9, 2017.

5 William Horobin and Francois De Beaupuy, "Macron Says France Must Regain Control of Some Energy Firms," *Bloomberg*, www.bloomberg.com, March 17, 2022.

6 On the exhaustion of investment in India: R. Nagaraj, "India Derailed: A Falling Investment Rate and Deindustrialisation," *India Forum*, www.theindiaforum.in, February 21, 2023; Vrishti Beniwal and Malavika Kaur Makol, "India's World-Beating Growth Hides Troubling Investment Trend," *Bloomberg*, www.bloomberg.com, January 11, 2022; and Abhishek Gupta, "India Insight: Post-Election, Revive Capital Expenditure or Risk Decline," *Bloomberg*, www.bloomberg.com, May 16, 2019.

7 Arjun Appadurai, "Modi and His Brand of Hindutva Are Direct Descendants of the British Raj and Its Policies," *The Wire*, https://thewire.in, December 13, 2021.

8 On the PRC's foreign policy stance, see Jake Werner, "The Sources of China's Vision for Global Economic Governance," Boston University Global Development Policy Center, www.bu.edu, September 9, 2021.

9 Pamela Engel, "'Ridiculous': Donald Trump Dismisses CIA Director's Stance Against Waterboarding," *Business Insider*, www.businessinsider.com, April 11, 2016. Trump's rocky relationship with the "intelligence community" began with his candor, scandalous for a Republican candidate at the time, about the U.S. invasion of Iraq, "one of the worst decisions in the history of the country," as he put it in 2016. Ian Schwartz, "Trump on Iraq: How Could We Have Been So Stupid? 'One of the Worst Decisions in the History of the Country'," *RealClearPolitics*, www.realclearpolitics.com, February 17, 2016.

10 Matthew Yglesias, Twitter, https://twitter.com, June 4, 2018. The tweet has since been deleted but screenshots of it can still be found.

11 Ho-Fung Hung, "The U.S.-China Rivalry Is About Capitalist Competition," *Jacobin*, https://jacobin.com, July 11, 2020.

12 Data taken from the U.S. Bureau of Economic Analysis series "Percent Change from Preceding Period in Real Gross Domestic Product," publicly available at www.bea.gov.

13 "Prototype Measures of Economic Well-Being and Growth," U.S. Bureau of Economic Analysis, www.bea.gov., accessed October 1, 2023.

14 Ibid.

15 Taken from the series "GDP Per Capita Growth (Annual Percent)" for OECD members and the world, publicly available at https://data.worldbank.org.

16 Branko Milanović, *Global Inequality: A New Approach for the Age of Globalization* (Cambridge, MA, 2016), p. 20.

17 Ibid., p. 24.

18 Ibid., p. 41.

19 Emmanuel Saez and Gabriel Zucman, "Wealth Inequality in the United States since 1913: Evidence from Capitalized Income Tax Data," *Quarterly Journal of Economics*, CXXXI/2 (May 2016), p. 551.

20 Ibid., p. 555.

21 Sean Wilentz, "No, There Is No Precedent," *Democracy Journal*, https://democracyjournal.org, 46 (Fall 2017).

22 "Politics, Populism, and the Life of the Mind: Sean Wilentz on Richard Hofstadter," *Journal of the History of Ideas*, www.jhiblog.org, July 27, 2020.

23 Robert Kagan, "This Is How Fascism Comes to America," www.brookings.edu, May 22, 2016.

24 There is nothing much new here: Lind's story is mostly a warmed-over retread of James Burnham's *The Managerial Revolution*, which has become a kind of rubric for reactionaries in the post-Trump era. Published in 1941, *The Managerial Revolution* claimed that private entrepreneurs had been replaced by a new stratum of intermediate

technocrats who had accrued all power and authority to themselves. Lind updates Burnham's thesis for the age of QAnon.

25   Thomas Ogorzalek, Spencer Piston, and Luisa Godinez Puig, "Nationally Poor, Locally Rich: Income and Local Context in the 2016 Presidential Election," *Electoral Studies*, LXVII (October 2020).

26   Shailly Gupta Barnes, "Waking the Sleeping Giant: Poor and Low-Income Voters in the 2020 Elections," available to download at www.poorpeoplescampaign.org, October 2021.

27   On the social bases of Trumpism, see Andrés Rodriguez-Pose, Neil Lee, and Cornelius Lipp, "Golfing with Trump: Social Capital, Decline, Inequality, and the Rise of Populism in the U.S.," *Cambridge Journal of Regions, Economy and Society*, XIV/3 (November 2021), pp. 457–81; Patrick Wyman, "It's Not Just Billionaires: Local Elites Also Dominate Our Society," *Jacobin*, www.jacobin.com, October 2021. Carter A. Wilson offers a broader historical explanation in *Trumpism: Race, Class, Populism, and Public Policy* (Lanham, MD, and London, 2021).

28   Franco Ferrari, "Italy's Poll Leader Says It's 'Conservative'—but Its Ideology Has Clear Fascist Elements," trans. David Broder, *Jacobin*, www.jacobin.com, August 16, 2022; Pietro Bianchi, "Italy's Lega is a Party of and for Business," trans. Chiara Migliori, *Jacobin*, www.jacobin.com, September 27, 2022.

29   Grzegorz Konat, "How Poland's Failed Transition Fed the Nationalist Right," *Jacobin*, www.jacobin.com, November 4, 2019; Maciej Gdula, "Poland's Far Right Is Distorting the Debate on Welfare—and Winning," *Jacobin*, interview, www.jacobin.com, July 16, 2020.

30   Sebastian Shehadi, "How German Automotive Investment in Hungary Exposes the Dark Reality of Globalisation," *Investment Monitor*, www.investmentmonitor.ai, October 8, 2021; Selam Gebrekidan, Matt Apuzzo, and Benjamin Novak, "The Money Farmers: How Oligarchs and Populists Milk the EU for Millions," *New York Times*, www.nytimes.com, November 3, 2019.

31   James Shotter, "Poland's Finance Minister Resigns after Backlash over Tax Reforms," *Financial Times*, www.ft.com, February 7, 2022.

32   Alberto Toscano, "The Nightwatchman's Bludgeon," *New Left Review*, https://newleftreview.org, October 29, 2022.

33   Adam Tooze, *The Wages of Destruction: The Making and Breaking of the Nazi Economy* (New York, 2005), ch. 4.

34   Ibid.

35   Martin Wolf, "Globalization Is Not Dying, It's Changing," *Financial Times*, www.ft.com, September 13, 2022.

3 Eclipse

1 The White House, "FACT SHEET: President Biden Sets 2030 Greenhouse Gas Pollution Reduction Target Aimed at Creating Good-Paying Union Jobs and Securing U.S. Leadership on Clean Energy Technologies," www.whitehouse.gov, April 22, 2021.

2 Alleen Brown, "Bipartisan Infrastructure Bill Includes $25 Billion in Potential New Subsidies for Fossil Fuels," *The Intercept*, https://theintercept.com, August 3, 2021; Ben Lefebvre, Catherine Boudreau, and Tanya Snyder, "Biden's Pro-Car, Pro-Gasoline Moves Leave Green Allies Fuming," *Politico*, www.politico.com, August 15, 2021; Hiroko Tabuchi, "Biden Administration Backs Oil Sands Pipeline Project," *New York Times*, www.nytimes.com, June 24, 2021.

3 Elizabeth Hagedorn, "Saudi Arabia's Defense of OPEC+ Cuts Draws Sharp U.S. Rebuke," *Al-Monitor*, www.al-monitor.com, October 13, 2022.

4 John Otis, "The U.S. Is Trying to Mend Ties with Venezuela. One Big Reason? Oil," NPR, www.npr.org, November 26, 2022.

5 David Agren, "U.S. and Canada Launch Trade Dispute with Mexico Over Clean Energy," *Financial Times*, www.ft.com, July 20, 2022. According to the report, "Mexico president Andrés Manuel López Obrador made light of the U.S.'s complaint at his morning press conference by saying 'nothing is going to happen.' He then played a song from Mexican artist Chico Che with the title: 'Oh, how scary!'"

6 Sanjeev Miglani, "India Rejects Net Zero Carbon Emissions Target, Says Pathway More Important," *Reuters*, www.reuters.com, October 27, 2021; Vrishti Beniwal and Malavika Kaur Makol, "India's World-Beating Growth Hides Troubling Investment Trend," *Bloomberg*, www.bloomberg.com, January 10, 2022.

7 For an extensive analysis and critique of the return of industrial policy, particularly so-called "Bidenomics" in the United States, see Jamie Merchant, "The Economic Consequences of Neo-Keynesianism," *The Brooklyn Rail*, https://brooklynrail.org, July 2023.

8 Leo Panitch and Sam Gindin, *The Making of Global Capitalism: The Political Economy of American Empire* (New York, 2012).

9 Marco Rubio, "We Need to Invest in America Again," *Washington Examiner*, www.washingtonexaminer.com, May 13, 2019.

10 Marco Rubio, "American Investment in the 21st Century," May 15, 2019, p. 25, available to download at www.rubio.senate.gov.

11 United Nations Conference on Trade and Development, "World Investment Report 2018: Investment and New Industrial Policies," https://unctad.org, 2018, ch. 4.

12 The European Parliament, "General Principles of EU Industrial Policy," *Fact Sheets on the European Union*, www.europarl.europa.eu, September 2022; Barbara Moens, Jakob Hanke Vela, and Jacopo

Barigazzi, "Europe Accuses u.s. of Profiting from War," *Politico*, www. politico.com, November 24, 2022; Paola Tamma and Samuel Stolton, "Revealed: France's Massive 'Made in Europe' Strategy," *Politico*, www.politico.com, January 13, 2023.

13 Bundesministerium für Wirtschaft und Klimaschutz, "Moderne Industriepolitik," www.bmwk.de, July 17, 2021.

14 William Horobin and Francois De Beaupuy, "Macron Says France Must Regain Control of Some Energy Firms," *Bloomberg*, www. bloomberg.com, March 17, 2022.

15 Mihir Sharma, "Modi Govt's Industrial Policy Shows It Has Run Out of Ideas and Is Taking India Back to Pre-1991," *The Print*, https:// theprint.in, July 16, 2021.

16 See Howard Brick, *Transcending Capitalism: Visions of a New Society in Modern American Thought* (Ithaca, NY, 2006), ch. 5.

17 Niall Ferguson and Moritz Schularick, "'Chimerica' and the Global Asset Market Boom," *International Finance*, x/3 (Winter 2007), p. 218.

18 Niall Ferguson, "The New Cold War? It's with China, and It Has Already Begun," *New York Times*, www.nytimes.com, December 2, 2019.

19 Jake Werner, "The Sources of China's Vision for Global Economic Governance," Boston University Global Development Policy Center, www.bu.edu, September 9, 2021.

20 Panitch and Gindin, *The Making of Global Capitalism*.

21 Ibid., ch. 8.

22 Michael Hudson, *Super Imperialism: The Origin and Fundamentals of u.s. World Dominance* (New York, 1972), p. 23.

23 Michael Hudson, "America's Neoliberal Financialization Policy vs. China's Industrial Socialism," blog, https://michael-hudson.com, April 14, 2021.

24 Matthew Klein and Michael Pettis, *Trade Wars Are Class Wars: How Rising Inequality Distorts the Global Economy and Threatens International Peace* (New Haven, CT, 2020), p. 7.

25 Ibid., p. 84.

26 The plainly tautological quality of the argument—wealthy elites decided to hoard wealth, because wealthy elites prefer to hoard wealth—follows from the general framework of the authors' analysis. Invoking a global balance sheet in which savings must equal investment at the aggregate level, it becomes necessary to choose a starting point for the causal sequence that motivates the trend of growing imbalances in an otherwise balanced world economy. In such a framework, that choice will inevitably be arbitrary. One could just as well start with the domestic conflicts that led to u.s. capital markets opening up to foreign investment and financing the federal budget deficit in the 1980s, as documented in Greta Krippner's

classic study of financialization, *Capitalizing on Crisis: The Political Origins of the Rise of Finance* (Cambridge, 2011).

27 Klein and Pettis, *Trade Wars Are Class Wars*, pp. 82, 64.

28 One wide-ranging study of introductory economics textbooks identifies a slew of different, inconsistent definitions of profit, none of which fit logically within the larger neoclassical system: Michele Naples and Nahid Aslanbeigui, "What *Does* Determine the Profit Rate? The Neoclassical Theories Presented in Introductory Textbooks," *Cambridge Journal of Economics*, xx/1 (January 1996), pp. 53–71.

29 Tilla Siegel, "Politics and Economics in the Capitalist World Market: Methodological Problems of Marxist Analysis," *International Journal of Sociology*, xiv/1 (Spring 1984), pp. 1–154.

30 Robert Allen, *Global Economic History: A Very Short Introduction* (Oxford, 2011), pp. 118ff.

31 Michael Howell, *Capital Wars: The Rise of Global Liquidity* (London, 2020), p. 46.

32 Data taken for China, the United States, and Germany from the World Bank series "Industry (including construction), value added (annual percent growth)," available at https://data.worldbank.org.

33 Panitch and Gindin, *The Making of Global Capitalism*, pp. 67–8.

34 Robert Brenner, *The Boom and the Bubble: The u.s. in the World Economy* (New York, 2002), p. 22.

35 This trade conflict was dramatized for the popular imagination in the classic action movie *Die Hard* (1988), in which the cop John McClane must defeat a German villain who takes hostages in a Japanese-owned skyscraper, "Nakatomi Plaza."

36 The World Bank, *World Bank Development Report 2020: Trading for Development in the Age of Global Value Chains*, www.worldbank.org, 2020, p. 15.

37 For an excellent overview of these transformations, see Ilias Alami and Adam Dixon, "Uneven and Combined State Capitalism," *Environment and Planning A: Economy and Space*, lv/1 (August 2021).

38 Caroline Freund, "The Global Trade Slowdown and Secular Stagnation," Peterson Institute for International Economics, www.piie.com, April 20, 2016.

39 Simon J. Evenett and Johannes Fritz, "Advancing Sustainable Development with fdi: Why Policy Must Be Reset," Centre for Economic Policy Research, https://cepr.org, June 2, 2021, p.17.

40 Ibid. Also see the World Bank, "fdi Watch: Quarterly Report," www.worldbank.org, 1/1, March 2021, p. 3.

41 On reverse development, see the classic work by Arghiri Emmanuel, who was already tracking similar dynamics in the 1960s: *Unequal Exchange: A Study of the Imperialism of Trade*, trans. Brian Pearce (New York, 1972).

42 Simon J. Evenett and Johannes Fritz, "Declining Foreign Direct Investment Can't Contribute Much to Sustainable Development," www.brookings.edu, June 3, 2021.

43 Ibid.

44 Germán Gutiérrez and Thomas Philippon, "Investmentless Growth: An Empirical Investigation," *Brookings Papers on Economic Activity* (Fall 2017), pp. 89–169.

45 Gustavo Grullon, Yelena Larkin, and Roni Michaely, "Are U.S. Industries Becoming More Concentrated?," *Review of Finance*, XXIII/4 (July 2019), pp. 697–743.

46 Ibid., p. 698.

47 Tony Smith, *Technology and Capital in the Age of Lean Production* (Albany, NY, 2000).

48 See Joel Rabinovich, "The Profit-Investment Puzzle under Financialisation: An Empirical Enquiry on Financial and Productive Accumulation by Non-Financial Corporations," Université Sorbonne Paris Cité, 2019, available at the HAL open access archive: http://theses.hal.science.

49 "No Way Forward, No Way Back: China in the Era of Riots," *Chuang* 1: *Dead Generations*, https://chuangcn.org, July 2016.

50 Phillip Neel, *Global China and the Global Crisis: Falling Profitability, Rising Capital Exports and the Formation of New Territorial Industrial Complexes*, doctoral dissertation, available at www.lib.washington.edu.

51 Ilaria Mazzocco, "Why the New Climate Bill Is Also about Competition with China," Center for Strategic and International Studies, www.csis.org, August 25, 2022; "U.S. Falls Into 'Isolationist Mentality' by Pushing Inflation Reduction Act to Curb China's New-Energy Rise," *Helsinki Times*, August 17, 2022.

52 Bureau of Labor Statistics, "Labor Productivity (Output per Hour): Manufacturing," 1987–2023, www.bls.org, accessed October 2, 2023.

53 Ibid., "Employment Projections – 2022-2023," www.bls.org, September 6, 2023; Lucia Mutikani, "U.S. Manufacturing Sector Slumps in October-ISM," *Reuters*, www.reuters.com, November 1, 2023.

4 The Money Theory of the State

1 Georg Friedrich Knapp, *Die Landarbeiter in Knechtschaft und Freiheit: Vier Vorträge* (Leipzig, 1891), p. 86.

2 J. M. Keynes, *The General Theory of Employment, Interest, and Money* (Boston, MA, 1964), p. 378.

3 Stephanie Kelton, *The Deficit Myth: Modern Monetary Theory and the Birth of the People's Economy*, ebook (New York, 2020), ch. 1. In the words of the economist and MMT forefather Abba Lerner, finance should be "functional," evaluated by its results on the economy, rather than "sound," shackled by arbitrary, self-imposed budget

limits. Abba Lerner, "Functional Finance and the Federal Debt," *Social Research*, x/1 (February 1943), pp. 38–51.

4 "What causes inflation? In almost all cases of large or persistent inflation, the culprit turns out to be the same—growth in the quantity of money. When a government creates large quantities of the nation's money, the value of the money falls." Gregory Mankiw, *Principles of Economics*, 6th edn (Mason, OH, 2008), p. 15.

5 "Recent Balance Sheet Trends," Board of Governors of the Federal Reserve System, www.federalreserve.gov, accessed January 11, 2022.

6 "Banks Lose Out to Capital Markets When It Comes to Credit Provision," *The Economist*, www.economist.com, July 25, 2020.

7 The simile is apt: by the end of 2022, observers were estimating that "zombie firms," companies that do not earn enough to service their debts and stay alive solely through easy access to credit, made up a fifth of the U.S. stock market. Robin Wigglesworth, "Cull of the Corporate Zombies," *Financial Times*, www.ft.com, October 27, 2022; Chris Giles, "Global Economy Enters Period of 'Synchronized Stagnation,'" *Financial Times*, www.ft.com, October 13, 2019; Lisa Lee and Tom Contiliano, "America's Zombie Companies Rack Up $2 Trillion of Debt," *Bloomberg*, www.bloomberg.com, December 16, 2020.

8 Committee for a Responsible Budget, "Covid Money Tracker," www.covidmoneytracker.org, last accessed February 14, 2023; Alicia Parlapiano et al., "Where $5 Trillion in Pandemic Stimulus Money Went," *New York Times*, www.nytimes.com, March 11, 2022.

9 Jerome Powell, "Monetary Policy and Price Stability," www.federalreserve.gov, August 26, 2022.

10 Carol Bertaut, Bastian von Beschwitz, and Stephanie Curcuru, "The International Role of the U.S. Dollar," FEDS *Notes*, www.federalreserve.com, October 6, 2021; Committee on the Global Financial System, "U.S. Dollar Funding: An International Perspective," CGFS *Papers*, no. 65, The Bank for International Settlements, www.bis.org, June 2020; Serkan Arslanalp, Barry Eichengreen, and Chima Simpson-Bell, "Dollar Dominance and the Rise of Nontraditional Reserve Currencies," IMF *Blog*, www.imf.org, June 1, 2022.

11 Prices have risen faster than workers' incomes throughout the post-pandemic inflation, making the notion of a "wage-price spiral" absurd. But absurdity typically isn't enough to dissuade economists from the truisms of economic theory. See Josh Bivens, "Wage Growth Has Been Dampening Inflation All Along—and Has Slowed Even More Recently," www.epi.org, May 12, 2022.

12 By mid-summer 2023, the Biden administration and its media pep squad were congratulating themselves for a strong U.S. economy, supposedly delivered by the president's economic program, and looking forward to a "soft landing" wherein the economy would

avoid a post-pandemic recession. The government's emergency policies during the pandemic provided a financial cushion for many households, allowing them to save much of the income that later would go toward consumption, which makes up about 70 percent of U.S. GDP. This consumption-led growth helped the United States to outperform much of the rest of the world in its post-pandemic recovery. But with consumers having spent down most of their pandemic-era savings, business bankruptcies rising, and the contractionary effects of higher interest rates yet to be fully felt, the U.S. recovery is on borrowed time.

13 "Real analysis proceeds from the principle that all the essential phenomena of economic life are capable of being described in terms of goods and services, of decisions about them, and of relations between them. Money enters the picture only in the modest role of a technical device that has been adopted in order to facilitate transactions . . . so long as it functions normally, it does not affect the economic process, which behaves in the same way as it would in a barter economy; this is essentially what the concept of Neutral Money implies. Thus, money has been called a 'garb' or 'veil' of the things that really matter . . . Not only can it be discarded whenever we are analyzing the fundamental features of the economic process but it must be discarded just as a veil must be drawn aside if we are to see the face behind it." Joseph Schumpeter, *History of Economic Analysis* (Abingdon, 2006), ebook, p. 277.

14 L. Randall Wray, *Modern Money Theory: A Primer on Macroeconomics for Sovereign Monetary Systems*, 2nd edn (New York, 2015), pp. 1–2.

15 Kelton, *Deficit Myth*, ch. 1.

16 Christine Desan, *Making Money: Coin, Currency, and the Coming of Capitalism* (Oxford, 2014), ch. 1.

17 Kelton, *Deficit Myth*, ch 1.

18 Friedrich Knapp, *The State Theory of Money* (*Staatliche Theorie des Geldes*) [1905], trans. H. M. Lucas and J. Bonar (London, 1924). Knapp is widely seen as a foundational figure in the MMT literature, and is cited frequently as such. However, even if he is not cited explicitly, his central argument that state acceptance establishes monetary value is at the cornerstone of all MMT discourse in its insistence that "taxes drive money." He also plays an important role in the sociologist Geoffrey Ingham's political theory of credit money in *The Nature of Money* (Cambridge, 2004).

19 On German economic development and monetary policy at the turn of the century, see Eric Hobsbawm, *Age of Empire* (New York, 1987), ch. 2; and Joyce Appleby, *The Relentless Revolution* (New York, 2010), ch. 6. For a more contemporary account, Max Weber's observations and analysis remain an excellent source. See his critique of Knapp, "Excursus: A Critical Note on the 'State Theory of Money,'" in

Economy and Society: An Outline of Interpretive Sociology, ed. Guenther Roth and Claus Wittich (Berkeley, CA, 1978), pp. 184–93.

20 As Max Weber observes with dismay in his commentary on *The State Theory*, "the work immediately was utilized in support of value judgements." *Economy and Society*, ed. Roth and Wittich, p. 184.

21 Knapp, *State Theory*, pp. 106–7.

22 Ibid., p. 111. See also L. Randall Wray, "From the State Theory of Money to Modern Monetary Theory: An Alternative to Economic Orthodoxy," *Levy Economics Institute*, Working Paper 792, p. 6.

23 Knapp, *State Theory*, p. 53.

24 Gerald Braunberger, "Was ist neu an der Modern Monetary Theory? Eine Erinnerung an Knapps Staatliche Theorie des Geldes," *Frankfurter Allgemeine Zeitung*, www.faz.net, January 18, 2012.

25 Knapp, *State Theory*, pp. viii–ix.

26 Erik Grimmer-Solem, *The Rise of Historical Economics and Social Reform in Germany, 1864–1894* (Oxford, 2003), ch. 3.

27 Knapp and his colleagues saw their project as "at once super-partisan and apolitical, and yet also deeply moral," as the historian Erik Grimmer-Solem describes it. "Central to that morality is the old liberal ideal of a classless, civil society." Grimmer-Solem, *Rise of Historical Economics*, p. 104.

28 Knapp, *Die Landarbeiter in Knechtschaft und Freiheit*, p. 86.

29 Geoff Mann, *In the Long Run We Are All Dead: Keynesianism, Political Economy, and Revolution* (New York, 2017).

30 Ibid., p. 53.

31 Keynes, *General Theory*, p. 293.

32 "Keynesian theory rests upon a speculative-financial paradigm—the image is of a banker making his deals on a Wall Street." Hyman Minsky, *John Maynard Keynes* [1975] (New York, 2008), p. 55.

33 "Close to 60 Percent of Surveyed Tech Workers Are Burnt Out—Credit Karma Tops the List for Most Employees Suffering From Burnout," *Blind Blog—Workplace Insights*, www.teamblind.com, May 29, 2018.

34 Tony Norfield, "Apple's Core: Moribund Capitalism," https://economicsofimperialism.blogspot.com, May 24, 2017.

35 "Money is not just *an* object of the passion for enrichment; it is *the* object of it. This urge is essentially *auri sacra fames* . . . the accumulation of money for the sake of money is in fact the barbaric form of production for the sake of production, i.e. the development of the productive powers of social labor beyond the limits of customary requirements." Karl Marx, *A Contribution to the Critique of Political Economy*, ed. Maurice Dobb (New York, 1970), p. 132.

36 "Why Wealth Matters: Years of Change," *Credit Suisse*, www.credit-suisse.com, October 10, 2019.

37 Kimberley Amadeo, "Why the U.S. Dollar Is the Global Currency," *The Balance*, www.thebalancemoney.com, July 23, 2020.

38 Serkan Arslanalp, Barry Eichengreen, and Chima Simpson-Bell, "Stealth Erosion of Dollar Dominance: Active Diversifiers and the Rise of Nontraditional Reserve Currencies," IMF *Working Papers*, www.imf.org, March 24, 2022.

39 "Market Value of Marketable Treasury Debt," FRED Economic Data, https://fred.stlouisfed.org, accessed December 20, 2023.

40 Oddný Helgadóttir, "Banking Upside Down: The Implicit Politics of Shadow Banking Expertise," *Review of International Political Economy*, XXIII/6 (December 2016), pp. 915–40. See also Daniela Gabor and Jakob Vestergaard, "Toward a Theory of Shadow Money," *Institute for New Economic Thinking*, Working Paper, April 2016.

41 "Banks Lose Out to Capital Markets When It Comes to Credit Provision," *The Economist*, www.economist.com, July 25, 2020.

42 To elaborate in a bit more detail: repo is a type of short-term contract in which, for a fee, a lender provides funds to a borrower on the basis of acceptable collateral, usually sovereign debt, which the borrower agrees to buy back later—often the next day, but sometimes up to several months after the initial deal. They allow institutional investors with large cash pools to earn a profit by lending to firms that hold a large amount of securities, such as banks, corporations, or hedge funds, but need cash to fuel further investment. Often mediated through a dealer seeking profit on the trade, repo allows them to swap collateral for cash; the firm taking the collateral can then, in turn, re-sell it forward to raise additional cash, fueling further credit creation throughout the financial system.

43 Committee on the Global Financial System, "Repo Market Functioning," Bank for International Settlements, www.bis.org, April 2017.

44 Daniela Gabor, "The (Impossible) Repo Trinity: The Political Economy of Repo Markets," *Review of International Political Economy*, XXIII/6 (December 2016), pp. 967–1000. See also Daniela Gabor and Cornel Ban, "Banking on Bonds: The New Links Between States and Markets," *Journal of Common Market Studies*, LIV/3 (May 2016), pp. 1–19.

45 Ibid., p. 3.

46 Lee and Contiliano, "America's Zombie Companies."

47 Ryan Niladri Banerjee and Boris Hofmann, "The Rise of Zombie Firms: Causes and Consequences," BIS *Quarterly Review*, www.bis.org, September 23, 2018.

48 Tommy Wilkes and Ritvik Carvalho, "$15 Trillion and Counting: Global Stimulus So Far," *Reuters*, www.reuters.com, May 11, 2020.

49 Ibid.

50 Eurostat, "Government Debt Down to 95.6 Percent of GDP in Euro Area," *Euroindicators*, https://commission.europa.eu, April 22, 2022.

51   Amanda Lee, "China Debt: How Big Is It and Who Owns It?," *South China Morning Post*, www.scmp.com, May 19, 2020.

52   S. Çelik, G. Demirtaş, and M. Isaksson, "Corporate Bond Market Trends, Emerging Risks and Monetary Policy," OECD *Capital Market Series*, 2020.

53   Andrea Shalal, "Global Debt Hits Record High of 331 Percent of GDP in First Quarter: IIF," *Reuters*, www.reuters.com, July 16, 2020.

54   For some thirty years the world has been expecting a "digital revolution" in productivity and economic performance that has yet to materialize. At this point, it is probably safe to conclude it never will. See Chris Giles, "Digitisation Failing to Lift Global Productivity, Study Shows," *Financial Times*, www.ft.com, April 14, 2019.

55   Patti Domm, "Falling Profit Margins Raise Some Alarm: 'It Can Be a Precursor to Layoffs and a Recession,'" CNBC, www.cnbc.com, October 21, 2019.

56   "Low Productivity Jobs Continue to Drive Employment Growth," OECD *Newsroom*, www.oecd.org, April 24, 2019.

57   Chris Giles, "Global Economy Enters Period of 'Synchronised Stagnation,'" *Financial Times*, www.ft.com, October 13, 2019.

58   Heather Long, "The U.S. Could Be on the Verge of a Productivity Boom, a Game-Changer for the Economy," *Washington Post*, www.washingtonpost.com, August 18, 2021.

59   The Conference Board, "Stagnant Productivity Growth Returns to the Post-Pandemic Economy: Labor Productivity Set to Flatline for the Second Straight Year in 2022, Dashing Hopes of Resurgence," Press Release, www.conference-board.org, April 29, 2022.

60   The Conference Board, "Global Economic Outlook," www.conference-board.org, February 2023.

5 Endgame

1   Jeremy C. Owens, "Corporate Profits Are Hitting Record Highs, But Earnings Expectations May Still Be Too Low," *MarketWatch*, www.marketwatch.com, July 2021.

2   Germán Gutiérrez and Thomas Philippon, "Investment-Less Growth: An Empirical Investigation," *Brookings Papers on Economic Activity*, 2017, p. 6.

3   Michael Smolyansky, "The Coming Long-Run Slowdown in Corporate Profit Growth and Stock Returns," FEDS *Notes*, www.federalreserve.gov, September 22, 2022.

4   According to the series "GDP Growth (Annual Percent) – High Income," taken from World Bank statistics, https://data.worldbank.org, accessed January 20, 2024.

5   "General Government Spending, Total, Percent of GDP," OECD Statistics, https://data.oecd.org, accessed January 20, 2024.

6 "Government Expenditure, Percent of GDP," IMF, www.imf.org, accessed January 20, 2024.

7 Jason Furman and Lawrence H. Summers, "A Reconsideration of Fiscal Policy in the Era of Low Interest Rates," www.brookings.edu, November 30, 2020, p. 9. Someone with a professional title like Furman's—the "Aetna Professor of the Practice of Economic Policy"—is sure to be an unbiased guide for understanding the economy.

8 Bryce Covert, "The Progressive Trio Shaping Biden's Ambitious Economic Policy," *New Republic*, https://newrepublic.com, May 4, 2021.

9 Mariana Mazzucato, *The Mission Economy: A Moonshot Guide to Changing Capitalism* (New York, 2021), ch. 6.

10 J. M. Keynes, *The General Theory of Employment, Interest, and Money* (Boston, MA, 1964), p. 159.

11 Greta Krippner, *Capitalizing on Crisis: The Political Origins of the Rise of Finance* (Cambridge, 2011), p. 4.

12 "The average annual growth of the global working-age population has decreased from 1.9 per cent in the period 1990–95 to 1.3 per cent in the period 2013–18; it is projected to fall even further, to 1.1 per cent, by 2030. This slowdown is reflected in a declining labour force growth, with the latter rate falling from 1.8 per cent in 1992 to below 1 per cent in 2018 and beyond . . . Employment growth has also decreased over the same period, from an average of 1.5 per cent in the 1990s to below 1 per cent 2018," *2019 World Social and Employment Outlook*, International Labour Organization, p. 7.

13 Fernand Braudel, *Civilization and Capitalism, 15th–18th Century*, vol. II: *The Wheels of Commerce*, trans. Siân Reynolds (Los Angeles, CA, 1992), p. 392.

14 Or alternatively, the value of a company's owned equity, or shares, equals its total assets minus its liabilities.

15 See Braudel, *Civilization and Capitalism*, vol. II; and Franklin A. Gevurtz, "The Historical and Political Origins of the Corporate Board of Directors," *Hofstra Law Review*, XXXIII/1 (January 2004), p. 116.

16 "For the rest, what is true of all forms of appearance and their hidden background is also true of the form of appearance 'value and price of labour,' or 'wages,' as contrasted with the essential relation manifested in it, namely the value and price of labour-power. The forms of appearance are reproduced directly and spontaneously, as current and usual modes of thought; the essential relation must first be discovered by science," Karl Marx, *Capital, a Critique of Political Economy*, vol. I, trans. Ben Fowkes (London, 1990), p. 682.

17 As an attempt to measure the cost of missed opportunities, the time value of money is basically an application of the economic concept of opportunity cost.

18　They can also represent a dramatic *reduction* of value, of course, if rates go the other way. Say the interest rate increases sharply, doubling to 10 percent. Then the price of the share in question halves, falling to $100.

19　There is a rich scholarly literature on operations research, but a good introduction to it—as part of a history of American postwar economics—can be found in Philip Mirowski, *Machine Dreams: Economics Becomes a Cyborg Science* (Cambridge, 2002). Harry Braverman and David Noble tie operations research to the scientific management of the labor process in *Labor and Monopoly Capital: The Degradation of Work in the Twentieth Century* (New York, 1974) and *Forces of Production: A Social History of Industrial Automation* (Milton Park, 1984), respectively. Lastly, see Paul Erickson et al., *How Reason Almost Lost Its Mind: The Strange Career of Cold War Rationality* (Chicago, IL, 2013), which situates the field within Cold War America's larger image of reason as a tool for optimizing calculation.

20　Bruce D. Grundy, "Merton H. Miller: His Contribution to Financial Economics," *Journal of Finance*, LVI/4 (August 2001), pp. 1183–206.

21　Donald MacKenzie, *An Engine, Not a Camera: How Financial Models Shape Markets* (Cambridge, 2006), pp. 46ff.

22　Perry Mehrling, *Fischer Black and the Revolutionary Idea of Finance* (Hoboken, NJ, 2005), p. 56; and MacKenzie, *An Engine, Not a Camera*, ch. 2. Incidentally, the author of a semi-recent book that claims to show how finance is nothing less than the engine of all human civilization, William Goetzmann, has a doctorate in—surprise!—operations research. See *Money Changes Everything: How Finance Made Civilization Possible* (Princeton, NJ, 2016).

23　MacKenzie, *Engine, Not a Camera*, pp. 61–3.

24　One of EMH's earliest forerunners was the fin-de-siècle French statistician Louis Bachelier, whose novel application of statistical techniques to security prices supposedly showed them to follow a series of unconnected stochastic movements that are not predictable based on past behavior.

25　Noble, *Forces of Production*, p. 55.

26　The essential text on Taylorism remains Braverman, *Labor and Monopoly Capital*.

27　James Boggs, *American Revolution: Pages from a Negro Worker's Notebook* (New York, 1963); Jason Smith, "The American Revolution: the George Floyd Rebellion, One Year Out," *Brooklyn Rail*, https://brooklynrail.org, July 2021.

28　Noble, *Forces of Production*, p. 30.

29　Ibid., chs 5 and 6.

30　I borrow the term "material abstraction" from Nancy Cartwright via Paul Mattick, *Theory as Critique: Essays on "Capital"* (Chicago, IL, 2019).

31 The global decline in the profit rate of industrial capital is by now a well-documented empirical trend. There are a variety of different methods for measuring it, and results differ slightly depending on the methods used. Likewise, the statistics collected by business organizations and government agencies do not directly represent the ratio Marx analyzed as the rate of profit, much less the more fundamental concepts of surplus value, variable capital, constant capital, and so on. But with these caveats, the general trend in contemporary measurements clearly indicates a long-term direction consistent with what one would predict based on the increasingly dense global concentration of production and a rising capital to labor ratio, or what Marx theorized as the organic composition of capital. For recent evidence, see Michael Howell, *Capital Wars: The Rise of Global Liquidity* (New York, 2020); Michael Roberts, "A World Rate of Profit—New Evidence," https://braveneweurope.com, 22 January 2022; Phillip Neel, "Global China, Global Crisis: Falling Profitability, Rising Capital Exports, and the Formation of New Territorial Industrial Complexes," dissertation, University of Washington, 2021. Even *The Economist* thinks the happy days of u.s. capitalism are likely behind us, recognizing that "the forces which fueled a decades-long rise in corporate earnings are petering out—or going into reverse." "Have Profits Peaked at American Businesses?," *The Economist*, www.economist.com, October 9, 2022.

32 These statistics are publicly available at the u.s. Bureau of Labor Statistics and the Bureau of Economic Analysis. Note that even here, the stagnant pattern in the u.s. government's statistics on domestic business investment are massively overinflated by an over-weighting of information processing and software in their measurements. This problem has been documented extensively. For a good overview, see the report "The Greater Stagnation: The Decline in Capital Investment is the Real Threat to u.s. Economic Growth," 2013, from the Information Technology and Innovation Foundation.

33 "Business Sector: Labor Productivity (Output per Hour) for All Employed Persons," Federal Reserve Economic Data, https://fred.stlouisfed.org, accessed October 2, 2023.

34 The Conference Board, "International Comparisons of Manufacturing Productivity and Unit Labor Costs—Data," December 2019 edition, www.conference-board.org.

35 u.s. Bureau of Labor Statistics, "Labor Productivity for Manufacturing Sector (Output per Hour)," 1987–2021, www.bls.gov; "Capital Productivity for Manufacturing Sector," 1987–2021, www.bls.gov, both accessed October 2, 2023.

36 "Non-Financial Corporations Debt to Surplus Ratio," oecd Data, https://data.oecd.org, accessed November 12, 2023. A condition of possibility for the financial bonanza over the last forty years has been

the secular decline in core interest rates over the same period. The Fed Funds Rate, which is the rate at which banks can borrow Federal Reserve deposits from each other overnight, has plummeted from nearly 20 percent in 1981 to basically zero. Falling or low interest rates are essential for sustaining the easy credit conditions necessary to inflate a fictitious capital boom. But the long downward fall of interest rates is only a secondary effect of the falling rate of profit, as the diminishing returns on long-term, profitable investment free up ever larger amounts of capital. All this excess capital needs to generate some kind of return wherever it can be found, pushing average rates for lending and borrowing downward. At the same time, the lack of investment demand puts a premium on other long-term assets that are considered safe, like Treasury bonds, driving their prices up and yields down. These trends produced a semi-permanent environment of low interest rates, which had indeed been hovering around zero since the Great Financial Crisis until the return of inflation in 2021. On the basis of data showing stagnating marginal returns on industrial capital in the United States and a precipitous fall of 50 percent in returns for China since the early 1980s, Michael Howell concludes that "falling industrial profitability and the associated structural shortage of safe assets are key factors behind the long downward slide in world interest rates," *Capital Wars*, p. 46.

37 The treadmill simile is taken from Moishe Postone, *Time, Labor, and Social Domination: A Reinterpretation of Marx's Critical Theory* (Cambridge, 1993), pp. 289–91, *passim*.

38 "Primary Dealers," Federal Reserve Bank of New York, www.newyorkfed.org, accessed January 20, 2024.

39 For further reading on this, see "Secondary Market Corporate Credit Facility," Board of Governors of the Federal Reserve System, www.federalreserve.gov, accessed January 19, 2024; Jeff Cox, "The Fed Is Buying Some of the Biggest Companies' Bonds, Raising Questions Over Why," CNBC, www.cnbc.com, June 29, 2020; Jeanna Smialek, "Fed Makes Initial Purchases in Its First Corporate Debt Buying Program," *New York Times*, www.nytimes.com, May 12, 2020.

40 Andrew Hauser, "From Lender of Last Resort to Market Maker of Last Resort Via the Dash for Cash—Why Central Banks Need New Tools for Dealing with Market Dysfunction," speech, www.bis.org, January 7, 2021.

41 Dawn Lim, "Index Funds Are the New Kings of Wall Street," *Wall Street Journal*, www.wsj.com, September 18, 2019.

42 Julie Segal, "History Made: U.S. Passive AUM Matches Active for First Time," *Institutional Investor*, www.institutionalinvestor.com, May 17, 2019.

43 See Benjamin Braun, "Asset Manager Capitalism as a Corporate Governance Regime," May 2021. Pre-print version of a chapter

published in J. S. Hacker et al., eds, *American Political Economy: Politics, Markets, and Power* (New York, 2021).

44 Annie Lowrey, "Could Index Funds Be 'Worse Than Marxism'?," *The Atlantic*, www.theatlantic.com, April 5, 2021; Scott Hirst and Lucian Bebchuk, "The Specter of the Giant Three," *Boston University Law Review*, XCIX/3 (May 2019), p. 721; Sahand Moarefy, "The New Power Brokers: Index Funds and the Public Interest," *American Affairs*, www.americanaffairsjournal.com, IV/4 (2020), pp. 3–18.

45 Jeanna Smialek, "Top U.S. Officials Consulted with BlackRock as Markets Melted Down," *New York Times*, www.nytimes.com, June 24, 2021.

46 Howell, *Capital Wars*.

47 "Labor Force Projections to 2024: The Labor Force Is Growing, But Slowly," U.S. Bureau of Labor Statistics, www.bls.gov, December 2015; Frank Tang, "China Population: Workforce to Drop by 35 million over Next Five Years as Demographic Pressure Grows," *South China Morning Post*, www.scmp.com, July 1, 2021.

48 "The U.S. Productivity Slowdown: The Economy-Wide and Industry-Level Analysis," Bureau of Labor Statistics, 2021, www.bls.gov, April 2021.

6 Becoming

1 Mario Tronti, *Workers and Capital* [1966] (London, 2019), p. xxvii.

2 "Twelve" refers to the twelfth letter of the English alphabet, "L," for "the law."

3 Matthew Impelli, "54 Percent of Americans Think Burning Down Minneapolis Police Precinct Was Justified after George Floyd's Death," *Newsweek*, www.newsweek.com, June 3, 2020.

4 Larry Buchanan, Quoctrung Bui, and Jugal K. Patel, "Black Lives Matter May Be the Largest Movement in U.S. History," *New York Times*, www.nytimes.com, July 3, 2020.

5 Amy Harmon and Sabrina Tavernise, "One Big Difference About George Floyd Protests: Many White Faces," *New York Times*, www.nytimes.com, June 12, 2020.

6 Karl Marx, *The Civil War in France*, ed. and trans. Terrell Carver (Cambridge, 1996).

7 Elle Lett et al., "Racial Inequity in Fatal U.S. Police Shootings, 2015–2020," *Journal of Epidemiology and Community Health*, LXXV/4 (April 2021), pp. 394–7; John Eligon and Shawn Hubler, "Throughout Trial Over George Floyd's Death, Killings by Police Mount," *New York Times*, www.nytimes.com, November 30, 2021; Sam Levin, "'No Progress' since George Floyd: U.S. Police Killing Three People a Day," *The Guardian*, www.theguardian.com, March 30, 2022. See also the "Mapping Police Violence" project at http://mappingpoliceviolence.us.

8 "With Whom are Many u.s. Police Departments Training? With a Chronic Human Rights Violator—Israel," Amnesty International, www.amnestyusa.org, August 25, 2016.

9 Emily Widra and Tiana Herring, "States of Incarceration: The Global Context 2021," Prison Policy Initiative, www.prisonpolicy.org, September 2021.

10 "Race and Ethnicity," Prison Policy Initiative, www.prisonpolicy.org, accessed January 10, 2023.

11 "United States Profile," Prison Policy Initiative, www.prisonpolicy.org, accessed January 10, 2023.

12 According to data compiled by the u.s. Bureau of Labor Statistics, www.bls.gov.

13 James Boggs, *American Revolution: Pages from a Negro Worker's Notebook* (New York, 1963), p. 85.

14 "Total Unemployed, Plus All Persons Marginally Attached to the Labor Force, Plus Total Employed Part Time for Economic Reasons, as a Percent of the Civilian Labor Force Plus All Persons Marginally Attached to the Labor Force," Bureau of Labor Statistics, www.bls.gov.

15 "Labor Force Participation Rate," Bureau of Labor Statistics, www.bls.gov. Some of this decline is accounted for by demographic factors like people retiring from the workforce, but over two decades of either decline or stasis indicates there are more forces at work.

16 As Mario Tronti puts it in *Workers and Capital*, trans. David Broder (New York, 2019), p. 188.

17 United Nations, "Sustainable Development Goal 11," 2018, https://unstats.un.org.

18 I take the horizontal/vertical axis from Anton Jäger and Arthur Borriello, "Left-Populism on Trial: Laclauian Politics in Theory and Practice," *Theory and Event*, xxiii/3 (July 2020), pp. 740–64.

19 Danny Schechter, "#OccupyNigeria Shows the Movement's Global Face," *Al-Jazeera*, www.aljazeera.com, January 23, 2012.

20 Max Fisher, "The Global Spike in Protests, Tracked in Social Media and Visualized," *Washington Post*, www.washingtonpost.com, October 15, 2012.

21 Thea Riofrancos and David Adler, "Gabriel Boric and Latin America's New Pink Tide," *New Statesman*, www.newstatesman.com, March 11, 2022. Toward the end of 2022 Peruvian President Pedro Castillo was ousted from office when he tried to dissolve congress and rule by emergency powers in response to charges of "moral incapacity" from congress, a legislative body almost universally despised by the entire country. This event set off a new wave of popular violence as the ousted president's supporters took to the streets to call for fresh elections, a demand supported by much of the rest of the country. Lethal state crackdowns have resulted in the deaths of at least 48 people in an uprising that is ongoing at the time of writing.

22 Martin Schoots-McAlpine, "Anatomy of a Counter-Insurgency: Efforts to Undermine the George Floyd Uprising," *Monthly Review*, https://monthlyreview.org, July 3, 2020.

23 Peter S. Goodman, "Why Chinese Companies Are Investing Billions in Mexico," *New York Times*, www.nytimes.com, February 3, 2023; Laura He, "China Is Still the Ultimate Prize that Western Banks Can't Resist," CNN *Business*, www.cnn.com, January 14, 2022.

24 International Labor Organization, *World Employment and Social Outlook*, 2019, p. 7.

25 Eli Friedman, "China in Revolt," *Jacobin*, www.jacobin.com, August 1, 2012.

26 Kathy Chu, Anjie Zheng, and Chun Han Wong, "China Wrestles With Wage Dilemma," *Wall Street Journal*, www.wsj.com, July 26, 2016.

27 Peter Wong, "How China's Pearl River Delta Went from the World's Factory Floor to a Hi-Tech Hub," *South China Morning Post*, www.scmp.com, October 6, 2015; Jason Jia-Xi Wu, "Chinese Regional Planning Under Xi Jinping: The Politics and Policy Implications of the Greater Bay Area Initiative," *Harvard Kennedy School Ash Center for Democratic Governance and Innovation Occasional Papers Series*, August 4, 2022.

28 OECD, "Gender Imbalances in the Teaching Profession," *Education Indicators in Focus*, 2017.

29 Alexia Fernández Campbell, "A Record Number of U.S. Workers Went on Strike in 2018," *Vox*, www.vox.com, February 13, 2019; U.S. Bureau of Labor Statistics, "25 Major Work Stoppages in 2019 Involving 425,500 Workers," Bureau of Labor Statistics, www.bls.org, February 14, 2020.

30 See Phil A. Neel, *Hinterland: America's New Landscape of Class and Conflict* (London, 2018).

31 Leo Tolstoy, *War and Peace*, trans. Constance Garnett (New York, 2002), Epilogue.

Acknowledgments

This book ended up taking longer than I anticipated. Partly this was due to rapidly changing world circumstances—I began writing in the fall of 2019—which is always a liability when writing a book about the present. But it is also due to a realization, about halfway into writing it, that if I wanted to do justice to the current moment I would need to go deeper into some of the theoretical issues than I had originally intended. Despite that decision, I have tried to keep the argument as accessible as possible for a general audience; whether or not I succeeded is up to readers to decide.

But acknowledgements must acknowledge, so here goes. Thanks are due first and foremost to Paul Mattick, without whom the book would not have been possible. Paul's steady encouragement throughout the entire process was a major motivator to keep pressing on, and his sympathetic but severe editorship of the project was instrumental in chiseling a bunch of unorganized thoughts into the finished work you hold in your hands. Amir Hernandez, Alex Gendler, Jordan Manalastas, Eli Wilkinson, and Eric White provided critical feedback, both stylistic and substantial, at key points in several of the chapters that strengthened them considerably. Years of conversations over drinks at Chicago pubs with Jake Werner, Chris Sherman, Tobita Chow, Ben Schacht, Tyler Zimmer, and David Hatch provided the intellectual background for many of the ideas explored in the book. I must also thank my partner, Gözde, whose truly impressive patience in supporting my ridiculous intellectual hobbies was crucial to the book's completion.

Lastly, this book is dedicated to my mother. Though she didn't live to see its publication, her love, kindness, and encouragement helped me to finish it. Thank you, mom.